A WEIRD UNFATHOMABLE ORDINARY

EVERYDAY LIFE

"Awakening is found in our pleasure and our pain, our confusion and our wisdom, available in each moment of our weird, unfathomable, ordinary everyday lives."

— Pema Chödrön

"A Weird Unfathomable Ordinary Everyday Life," by William Bridges and Dianne Jenkins. ISBN 978-1-60264-480-9.

Published 2009 by Virtualbookworm.com Publishing Inc., P.O. Box 9949, College Station, TX 77842 Text ©2009 William Bridges and Dianne Jenkins. All Dianne Jenkins art ©2009 Dianne Jenkins unless otherwise noted. All rights reserved. No part of this publication may be reproduced, stored in a retrieval system, or transmitted in any form or by any means, electronic, mechanical, recording or otherwise, without the written permission of William Bridges and Dianne Jenkins.

Manufactured in the United States of America

A WEIRD UNFATHOMABLE ORDINARY EVERYDAY LIFE

A MAIL-ART CONVERSATION:

WILLIAM BRIDGES & DIANNE JENKINS

All day the flowers and painting

have accompanied each other

beside my desk, recalling Tozan's words,

how cloud and mountain are son

and father, how they rely

on each other in perfect freedom.

Without the mountain, the flowers

would pass unnoticed,

because of the flowers I see the fall

of water, and the lone boatman lowers

his line again into the abyss.

A Note at the Beginning

This book records a friendship in art and words, pursued since 2006 between Dianne Jenkins, an artist in Massachusetts, and me, an Indiana writer and poet. (We also share a tangential family connection.) The letters are excerpts, edited lightly to remove a few references that might be hurtful or infringe the privacy of others.

Dianne's illustrated letters are wonderful gifts, launched on the tide of the U.S. Mail with no assurance they will get through intact—although the post office is actually quite accommodating, to a point, of items that defeat its automated machinery.

Ordinarily, "mail artists" like Dianne never see their work again. To borrow a Buddhist comment about life, "it is like heading out into the ocean in a boat you know is going to sink."

There are communities of mail and rubber-stamp artists, to which Dianne has belonged in the past. Several pieces of her work are included in a book, *Rubber Soul*, by Sandra Mizumoto Posey (University Press of Mississippi, 1996). One of these pieces, a self-portrait in a mask, appears in the next column. A writer in *Rubber Soul* commented that "the raw intimacy of [Dianne's] pieces consistently inspires admiration and a sense of connection with the artist." And a member of her mail-art group added that the artists "feel closest to Dianne Jenkins, despite the fact that she is one of the members fewest of the others have actually met."

Some mail artists simply exchange their work. Dianne writes letters—forthright, often eloquent, occasionally desperate. She works by creating a decorative "frame" and then filling it with appropriate words. Like the sage Tozan's cloud and mountain, the letters and the art are independent, but rely on each other. In preparing this book, I also discovered that excerpting the art with a nearby line or two of handwriting often produced something surprising and new.

Finally, as a poet, I was struck by the way Dianne makes connections that are unexpected, unusual, and right. I would know her voice anywhere, and I'm happy to be in this book with her.

—Bill Bridges

Dianne is married to David, the son of my father's third wife, Marie. I knew Marie forever—she saved my life as a child, something I've written about in a memoir, Under the Heaven Tree. David and I grew up together, and it did not seem at all unusual that in their sixties, after the deaths of spouses, Jack (my father) and David's mother, Marie, should marry.

With that family connection established, I saw David and Dianne occasionally—at Jack's summer cabin in Robinson, Illinois, or (after his death) at Marie's home in Anderson, Indiana. But these meetings were infrequent. David and Dianne lived in a big house in Swampscott, Massachusetts, a short walk from the ocean, and didn't come west often. So, in a way, I didn't really meet Dianne or encounter her as an artist until my son Colin and I went to Swampscott in 2006 for Marie's memorial service (her Gone to Glory Party, as Dianne put it). It was good to see David and sit up late at night remembering our shared childhood. And to browse among Dianne's fabric dolls, rubber-stamp art, and illustrated scrapbooks. And to meet Anne, a teacher who shares their home.

I exchanged an e-mail or two with David later. "I am delighted that you are in my life," he wrote. "You and Dianne are a gift in my life, too," I responded.

But the correspondence that led to this book began with a table . . .

To Bill

There is a little table, the one your father made, that you mention in your first book. A little scalloped-edge one that is on the 3rd floor here. I didn't think about it until after your visit. Next time I'll send a photo, and if you want it we will find a way for you to get it.

I'm sorry it took me a while to respond to your lovely note. That's just the way life is these days. About 20 years ago, I was into MAIL-ART and spent all my creative energy on making things to send in the mail to other artists who would make things to send back. Going to the mailbox was such a treat during those 8 or 10 years. But I gave that up and now on the rare occasion that I write to someone it is a little project that I thoroughly enjoy.

Since death alone is certain and the time of death is uncertain what should I do?

I've been pondering the question for a few years now, wondering if what I am doing is the "right" thing for me to be doing. I had a teacher, once, in a bookmaking class, who talked about art having "POW"—something about clear meaning—obvious—hit you in the face kind of thing. Half the time I'm not clear what my art is saying and the idea of meaning, like am I supposed to have a deep message,

TO:
WILLIAM A. BRIDGES
920 WALNUT STREET
FRANKLIN IN
46131

worries me. I like the idea that "mountains should be climbed with as little effort as possible." I can see how that applies to life and to art, writing and making things of all sorts. "Without desire" seems harder to me. From what I know of Buddhism (which is not a huge amount) I understand that desire is the central cause of suffering in the world and that getting rid of it is not an easy task.

It's a beautiful day and as I pause to look up I see the buds getting fat on the apricot tree and I think we'll have flowers next week for Easter.

To Dianne

There is no way you could have known that your illustrated letter would drop in the mailbox today, on my 71st birthday—a wonderful present. "Synchronicity," a New Jersey writer friend calls such things. I'm almost speechless at getting such a gorgeous work of art.

I think the idea that art has to have a clear meaning in the sense of hitting you in the face is simply wrong. I can wonder around in your letter for a long time (I wrote "wonder" when I meant "wander"—it's both), seeing things I missed the first time,

enjoying your particular take on things. Isn't that what a piece of art is really supposed to do?

I think the Buddhist approach does help. You may know Shunryu Suzuki's popular *Zen Mind, Beginner's Mind*. It's an easy-reading, unpretentious book, but it makes good points. I imagine Suzuki would say something like, "Well, you can't really get rid of desire and so you'll still suffer, but here are some thoughts on how to live in spite of this." He says it much better, of course. I read recently that as he was dying (of cancer) he looked up at a friend and said, "I don't want to die." The point of the story was that he was speaking truthfully, but not desperately, just stating a fact. (He also said that "if you lived forever, you would really have a problem.")

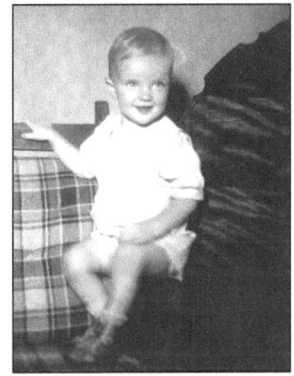

I was intrigued by your mention of the "pie-crust" table. Don't know for sure if the one you have is the one mentioned in *Under the Heaven Tree*, but I believe you can see enough in the enclosed photo to tell. The table is almost mythic—finding it again

I bought a wooden whistle
But it wooden whistle.
So I bought a steel whistle,
But it steel wooden whistle.
Then I bought a tin whistle
and now I TIN WHISTLE!

would be like reclaiming a piece of my childhood. (When I put a different picture of this adorable child into *Under the Heaven Tree*, a friend said, "C'mon, you were never that sweet. You hired some child to pose for that.")

Gosh, I've got three more lines on this page. A haiku maybe?

Dianne's letter. Spring
dynamiting my mailbox
and raining flowers.

APRIL
18

To Bill

Tomorrow my 5-year-old grandson will be here for a visit and in mid-May we will have the intense company time when my son Nicholas comes from Paris with his daughters Emma aged 6 and Pauline aged 4.

They will visit for 3½ weeks while their Mom, Nick's wife Laurence, enjoys her last month in Paris alone before they move to Dubai. (Nick has taken some new work there after his previous job in Paris.) After that a friend from California will stay for a week and after that Anne & I are going to lie on the beach and read novels.

Meanwhile here are some photos of the table. It is 30" across. I am sad to part with it but from the sentimental meaning it has for you I certainly think you should have it. Let me know how you want to get it from here to there.

APRIL
24

To Dianne

Dearest Dianne,

Your offer of the "piecrust table" took my breath away—and it is The Table. On consideration, though, I think it's right where it should be, in your house, a reminder of Jack. Maybe I'll come visit it sometime!

It was a temptation, though. It stirred all my latent (sometimes not so latent) acquisitiveness. But I'm 71 years old and we

GIVING=GETTING

have to leave all these beautiful things—I'm practicing.

I loved your letter. Everything got through the mail just fine. Opening one of your letters requires a sharp knife and the approximate level of care required to unpack a Dead Sea Scroll. And I save the envelopes!

Much love to you and Dave.

 *To Bill*

Today is like an early summer day. I have been to the beach and put my feet into the refreshing (icy) water and it is so sweet to be outside without coats and gloves.

Anne, my best lady partner, and I went to Philadelphia last weekend for a convention (of teachers in her field) but we

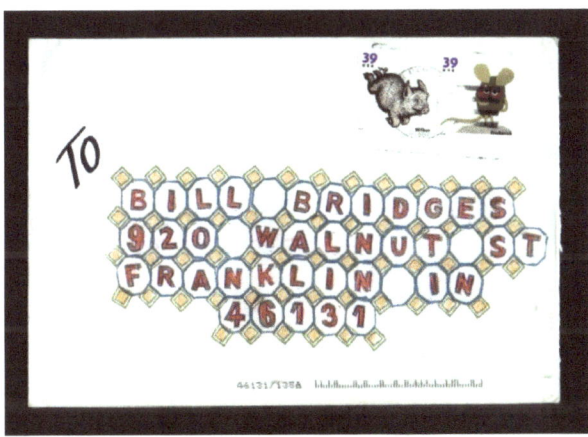

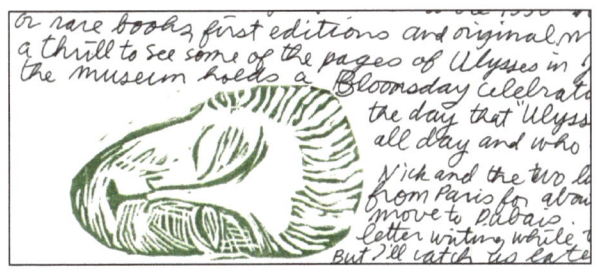

spent most of the weekend poking around in odd museums and at used book stores and thrift shops. At one of the libraries in Penn we found this wonderful quotation, in a stained-glass window: "O Blessed Letters! That combine in one/All ages past and make one live in all/You we do confer with who are gone/And the dead living into counsel call."

We had a tour of a small museum—the Rosenbach—where these two brothers who lived from the 1870s to the 1950s have a huge collection of rare books, first editions, and original manuscripts. It was quite a thrill to see some of the pages of *Ulysses* in Joyce's handwriting. And the museum holds a Bloomsbury celebration each year on June 16, the day that *Ulysses* is set on. They read all day and who knows what else.

[Enclosure about the Barnes Museum near Philadelphia.]

To Dianne

I'm on the verge of a familiar error—that of setting aside a letter I really like, to be answered at leisure, and then of course the leisure doesn't come. Pretty soon three months have passed, the correspondent feels abandoned, and it's all over.

Well, not this time! And you are excused from answering right away, because I know Nick and the girls will be there. So have a

i'd better finish the first write-up before Nick + the picture i prep gets going again?

Maybe I should get a job but what kind of work could I actually do?

today is so beautiful look at the leaves coming out.

our lives are very good.

i'd better get going before the p.o. closes.

I wonder what we will have for dinner tonight.

Do we have to stay for the whole set tonight?

I hear feet coming upstairs, it must be David.

I'm thirsty. where's that glass of ice water?

Francis Picabia and the Dada artists feel so current.

There is a coffee stain below this circle. maybe I'll color it.

I dreamed of phones. I couldn't dial again last night.

Everyone needs me to do their shit work.

I'm tired.

"our heads are round so that our thoughts can change direction."
Francis Picabia

Me

ME

ME

IT'S ALL ABOUT ME

"our heads are round so that our thoughts can change direction."
Francis Picabia

6

wonderful time with them, and fill me in later.

Your letters, and this is a great virtue, do require some time to think about, re-read, and excogitate upon. (I think this is the first time in my life I have used that word, but it describes the process exactly—something more than simply thinking about, an active consideration and response.)

The Penn window! What wonderful lines! *Bartlett's* was no help, but Google produced the work and author instantly: *Musophilus*, Samuel Daniel (aka Sam. Danyel), 1562-1619.

I loved the letter and the nosegay of thoughts (especially "What should I write to Bill about?") And then I had to google Francis Picabia, another shocking gap in my knowledge. He's amazing! Where has he been all my life? You know, because you are not an unconscious artist, the difficulty of constructing a montage of seemingly ordinary thoughts in a way that lifts them out of the ordinary—what you've written is quite a nice, circular "concrete" poem.

You enclosed material about the Barnes Museum, and I may actually try to get to it next month when I'm in the Philadelphia area on a working assignment. Will also check to see if the Rosenbach is in commuting distance. It would be fun to see *Ulysses* in Joyce's handwriting; he's been on my mind while reading a pretty tedious biography of Ezra Pound. Am now convalescing with murder mysteries.

Don't know if I've said much about my rain book, titled *A Fine Smirr of Rain*, from the Scottish word for mist. When I say I'm writing a book about rain, most people respond, "Huh?" So I've taken to saying that it's really about life and the natural world, with rain as a metaphor. That makes it sound respectable, but heck, I just wanted to write a lot about rain.

Do you think it's possible, Dianne, that we might collaborate eventually on a writing/art project? What shape it would take is still unclear to me, and there is no urgency—I think the danger is in trying to suggest in advance what it might be. The wife of an acquaintance decided with a friend that they would write to each other every week for a year and then publish the correspondence. The result was interesting, but a little too contrived for my taste. I want things to happen naturally, or else not to happen.

"Our lives are very good," your nosegay says. "Maybe I should get a job but what kind of work would I actually do?" It's

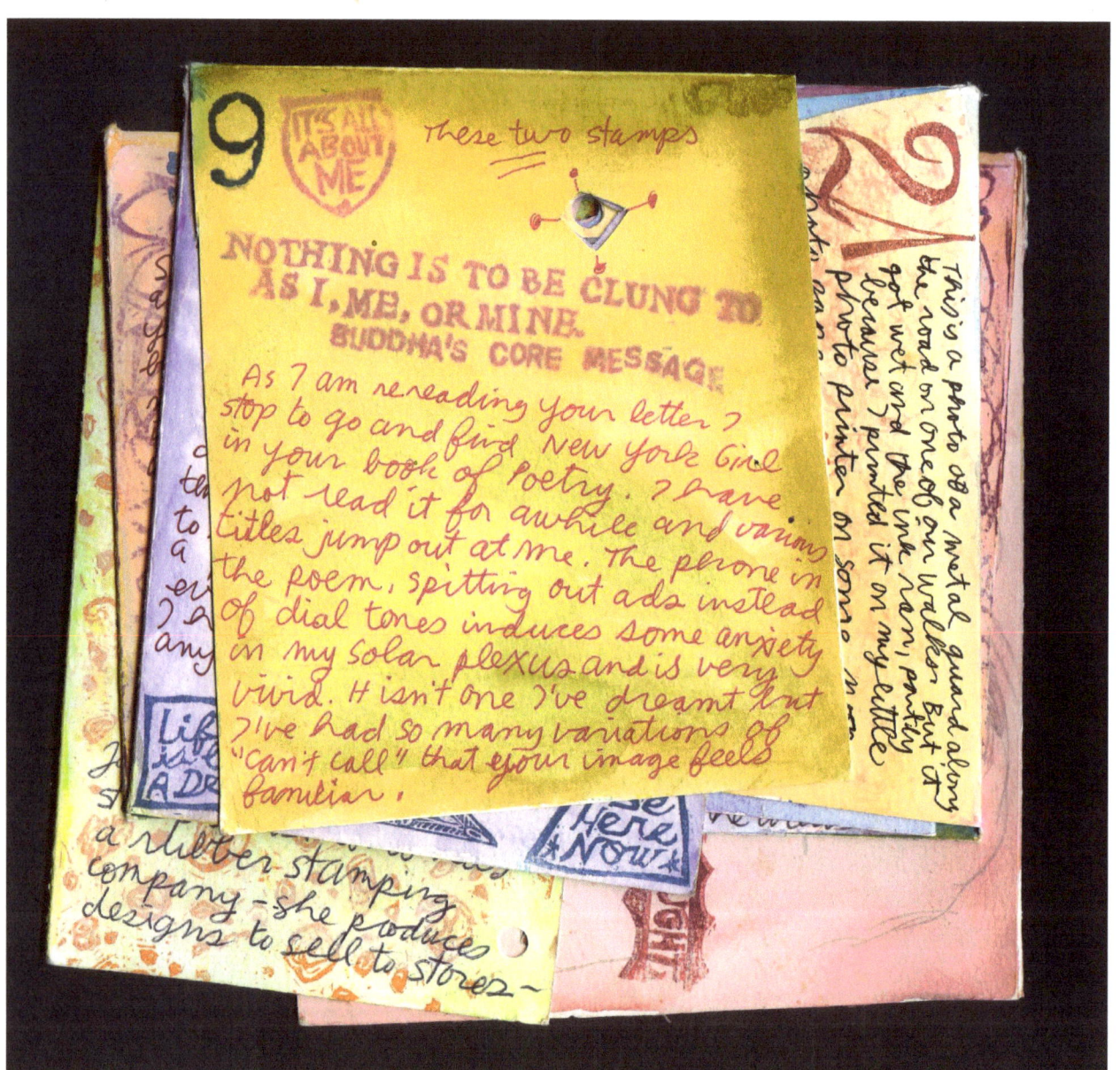

9 IT'S ALL ABOUT ME

these two stamps

NOTHING IS TO BE CLUNG TO
AS I, ME, OR MINE.
BUDDHA'S CORE MESSAGE

As I am rereading your letter I
stop to go and find New York Girl
in your book of poetry. I have
not read it for awhile and various
titles jump out at me. The phone in
the poem, spitting out ads instead
of dial tones induces some anxiety
in my solar plexus and is very
vivid. It isn't one I've dreamt but
I've had so many variations of
"can't call" that your image feels
familiar.

This is a photo of a metal guard along
the road on one of our walks. But it
got wet and the ink ran, pretty
neat when I printed it on my little
photo printer on some m—

a rubber stamping
company — she produces
designs to sell to stores —

Life is A DREAM

HERE NOW

8

occurred to you, I'm sure, that you're doing it. I'm beset with some of the same thoughts. What am I going to do when I grow up? I dunno, so I keep writing what occurs to me, and making the garden, and enjoying life with Karen and the cats. My *Bartlett's* does, in fact, have some quotes from Sam. Danyel, though not the wonderful one. Among other things, he said, "This is the thing that I was born to do."

Much love to you, David, and all your house.

 *To Dianne*

I have been to the Barnes Museum, and it was just as odd and wonderful as you said it would be. It wasn't easy to get there, and I understand I was quite lucky to get a same-day reservation. Had to ride a bus for an hour and a half each way from King of Prussia, and make a mid-point transfer, but it was worth it (and I got to ride free by flashing my Medicare card—no wonder the transit system is going broke).

Wotta place! I'm enclosing a piece from the *New Yorker* about the Barnes in which the author writes that he felt "momentarily possessed of a secret that might save the world, on the impossible condition that I could understand it." I had a similar epiphany—the feeling that I was on the verge of understanding what it was about these colored scraps of canvas that makes them priceless. That feeling may have come in the big room (you'll remember it) where I was completely alone with Rousseau's "Nude and Bear" and other masterworks. But the secret eluded me just as it did the *New Yorker* guy.

I always jot notes in art museums, and I see that I was overdosing on Renoir after about the 18th bathing beauty, and had to have a Cezanne infusion.

Alas, the museum is not long for its present site. The move to downtown Philly appears a done deal, even though the locals are still grumbling. A replica is planned, with everything just as Mr. Barnes hung it—but it won't be quite the same, and thanks to you I got to see the original.

'To Bill

[A foldout letter of 24 pages, extending to a foot and a half by two feet, written on both sides]

I have been getting ready to write to you for a while. I cut & folded this paper and began to play with it, but then it never "felt together," so I have finally decided it's time to begin writing anyhow.

A friend of ours, a Japanese-American stamp artist, was here for about a week recently and told us about seeing a psychic who suggested she stand on a chair for 10 minutes a day and do it for 60 days in a row. If you miss a day you have to start over. So Anne and I have each been doing this, and now we are on day 11. I don't know why I am starting a letter this way, but here it is.

Over the years, David and I have been involved in a number of "new age spiritual groups" and have done a fair amount of meditation, but somehow this standing on a chair is really capturing me. LAUGH AT IT At any rate, it has brought up all sorts of dilemmas, like how to be present without being run around by my thoughts, emotions, and my physical energy.

I stopped here to try to figure out how to unfold this. LAUGH AT IT I have gotten into the habit of carving words that I want to think about or that seem important to remember. Then I go through a period of stamping them on everything, like the one about death being certain, but the time uncertain. I have never come to any clear answer.

O.K., I got that out of my system for the moment. Hello, Bill, how are you? What's new? Here's a photo of my little French girls looking sweet— in actuality we were in downtown  Gloucester and they were barreling down the brick sidewalks with their pousettes [doll strollers], terrifying old ladies. After that we went to a beach where both girls got naked and were extremely wild.

I just took some time off from this letter to mess with my sewing machine. The funny

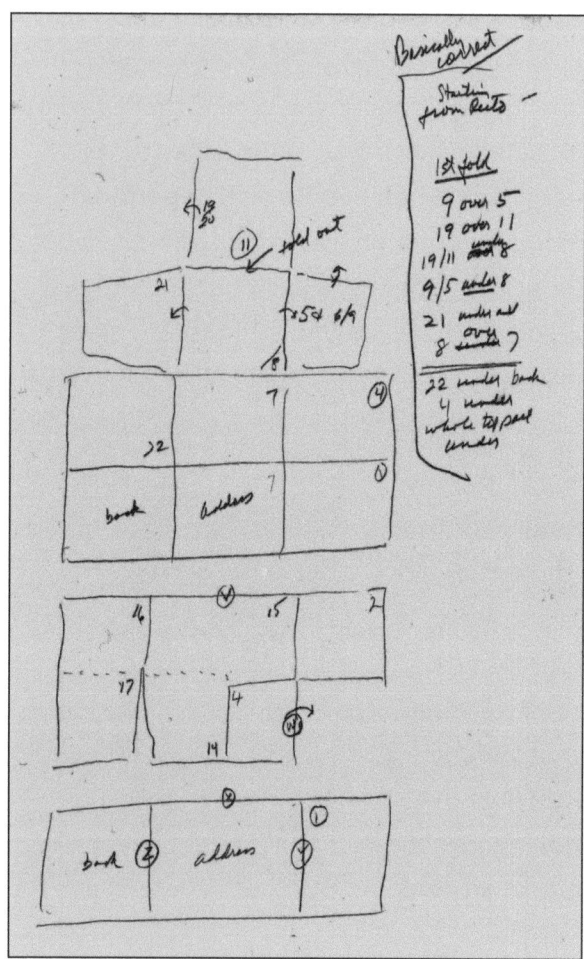

⇧ **Bill's scheme for folding the big letter**

thing about a letter is that you don't know that I left unless I tell you. I've been having trouble with the sewing machine and was inclined to just have David pick up one at Costco, but they didn't have any in stock so I got out the manual and took the thing apart

and cleaned it out and oiled it and I think it will be fine. I have two "dolls" in process. I have developed different ways of making them, but I forget each time how I did it before so they are all made differently.

As I try to make this thing unfold it feels more chaotic. I'm sorry for the confusion of this letter. Next time I will choose a simpler form. The word chaos keeps coming up to remind me of when I was standing on the chair this morning out on the deck, staring at the tangle of branches on the apricot, branches that need pruning. I thought how concerned I am with TIDYING UP THE CHAOS. It may be a hopeless task and is the chaos really more ordered than it seems? I know people who are into chaos theory but I don't know much about it. Do you?

Next week David, Anne & I are taking a long weekend in NYC. We'll have to see if Colin can meet us for dinner. There are lots of art things we want to see while we're there. What I like the very most are the odd obsessive artists—the Brooklyn museum has the work of a woman from Columbus who made her work out of natural & synthetic materials including twigs, rags, pig grease! etc. Another one I like is some sculptures by Nek Chand, a government worker in India who built a "city" in the

wilds by carrying materials there each night on his bicycle. When officials found out about it after a number of years, they threatened to dismantle it but it has come to be a treasured "OUTSIDER ART ENVIRONMENT." A few of his pieces are on display at the folk art museum in New York although we would really like to go to Chandigarh, India, to see the 25-acre deal.

Your book about rain appeals to me; I do love my sunny days sitting in my old beach chair in the soft sand listening to the sound of waves tumbling onto the shore over and over again, but I would definitely miss the sound of a hard rain on the roof, the feel of the tiny smooches of water on a misty morning as I walk the dog over again to the beach where the seagulls dive and fling crabs on the sand and then fly up with their lonely cry.

The sun is high up now and David and Anne have arrived from their "real-world work," so I'll go unpack groceries and write more later.

* * *

Over the years I have been part of exchanges through the mail and some sort of round-robin things where someone sends an art piece that you add to and send on. I have no idea about how you and I might collaborate but I am happy to keep the exchange going and see if some ideas develop. I judge myself as someone who does not stick to things in depth. I do stick to things in time. I am on my 5th year of doing a daily page for a visual journal and Anne has been doing it too for 4 of the years. But I wonder if there is something else.

My life is so deeply involved with the people here and their needs that I am sometimes afraid that if I get too involved in something they will feel abandoned, that I will not take care of them properly. As I write this I can see this has a direct correlation to the old Mom & ME relationship. My mother committed suicide when I was in my early 20s. And like most people in that situation, I battle the idea that I could/should have done something to save her.

Here is a photo of a metal guard along the road on one of our walks, but it got wet and the ink ran, partly because I printed it on my little photo printer on some non-photo paper. I like to make things and could endlessly create just for the pleasure of it. I guess in the end I have to agree with your Sam Danyel: **This is the thing that I was born to do.**

 ·*To Dianne*

[Bastille Day] This is not really a letter—just an acknowledgment that your magnificent foldout made it safely through the mails. In fact the post office pasted on a little strip of bar code at an appropriate spot on the front, thereby becoming a co-creator (sort of). I would just add that short missives have a perfectly good place. This is so you won't think I'll be disappointed if the next letter is not a 48-page foldout.

Well, I seem to have started a letter, so I'll tell you what's on my mind. Karen and I were at my brother Charles's on Tuesday, and he had brought home from the library a handsome volume about the touring King Tut exhibition. All very nice. But one photo jumped out and grabbed me—a flash powder exposure in an antechamber of the tomb before it was cleared, showing an incredible jumble of Pharaonic bric-a-brac. It scared me slightly, it seemed so recent, without any museum distancing. Something demanded to be written, if I could sort out what it was. The enclosed draft is at least a first stab, no critical comment sought. (The Necropolis Police did exist—they patrolled the Valley of the Kings for centuries, but of course the system eventually broke down and tomb robbers got most of the stuff.)

The Attic

*Tutankhamen's corpse came into Cairo
as salted fish—the Customs had
no category for mummies.*

*This was 1923. Its finders cleared the tomb
and took pictures. The fabulous gold
was there, the nested sarcophagi,*

*but one photo shows an anteroom that looks
like nothing so much as someone's attic,
piled ceiling-high with junk.*

*It's understandable—so little space to store
all the necessities for an afterlife
befitting godhead, so chests*

*were heaped on each other like cardboard boxes,
chariot wheels packed in against them
for re-assembly on the other shore,*

*and the odd chair or table thrown
without ceremony onto the pile,
immortal trash. But how real it seems,*

*this unrehearsed evidence kept under seal
for aeons by the Necropolitan Police,
and ordinary, the sad jumble of death.*

To Bill

We are just back from 4 days in NYC and we saw so much interesting and inspiring stuff. We actually went to 11 museums but it didn't feel a strain. In the end, of course, some of the best things were serendipitous. One time we rode past the NY public library on a bus and Anne had never been in there and said she'd like to go if we had time. The next day we went to see some work at the International Photography Museum, and Lo & Behold we were practically next door to the library. A docent was giving a tour and she recommended that we see the Declaration of Independence. We said, "Okay," and somehow when we got in that room we were all fascinated and touched. I actually cried and I think of myself as a tough old bird. David cried too but he is a softy. What they had on display was

Jefferson's original handwritten first draft and then various original printed versions. We saw the first one that was printed on July 5th by a printer who stayed up all night to get it done, and we realized that in those days it took time for the news to travel and then there would be another version printed in Philadelphia and a few days later one in New York. It all became so immediate and real, that these were real people just like us.

In front of Lincoln Center was a large sculpture made of maybe 30 boats, like a huge metal flower. One night we were there while there was swing dancing going on on the plaza with all kinds of couples—children & parents, old old people and young hipsters dancing away in the hot night.

We are leaving here on August 3rd to head towards Kansas, where Anne's family lives.

P.S. Anne has been collecting old typewriters from yard sales. That's what I used for the address label.

JULY 28

To Dianne

This is still not a letter, but just a quick response to your last one, with the Declaration of Independence. With luck this may barely reach you before you head west.

I thought at first that you wrote Anne was collecting old "typewriting" from yard sales, but I think now you wrote "typewriters," which is more likely. I wonder what kind she has—I barely missed a Blickensderfer once.

Have a good trip. You're welcome if you're in the neighborhood.

AUGUST 14

To Dianne

It was a joy to have you here. I really can't express how touched I was that you brought the piecrust table. It's such an icon to me—I just sit on the couch and gaze at it, and think about my dad making it, probably in the '20s or early '30s. By now it needs a little careful restoration, and we know whom to have do it—furniture experts at Homer, Indiana, who did some work for us on a desk of dad's that had gotten in bad shape. They're slow, which is good. After about six months, we went over to visit the desk, but it was still "in 1,300 pieces," the owner said. Karen said, "Just be sure you get them all back," and he smiled and said, "You'll never know." (He got them all in—we think—and it's beautiful.) But there's no hurry with getting the table to him—I just want to have it around for a while, as a reminder of dad, and of your thoughtfulness.

Other things going on. Did I tell you I was reading the *Iliad*, at 10 pages a day? This is the secret, I've discovered, for getting through long classics—just do the 10 pages and quit for the day. Pretty soon you're finished. With this system I have marched through the *King James Bible* and the *Decline and Fall of the Roman Empire*. I started the *Iliad* in March, but was in danger of quitting despite the plan, because Homer is so damn violent and bloody it was driving me into depression. So I started alternating the 10 pages with a re-reading of Shunryu Suzuki's *Zen Mind, Beginner's Mind*, which alleviates the pain.

When I got your 12-fold letter back in July, I spread it out, measured it, plotted the coordinates of the holes you had made in it (for the binding string), and devised a plan for getting it refolded properly. I also read it!

At the time, you and Anne were standing on chairs, which struck me as an excellent idea, a sort of Zen practice. I hope you were able to get the 60 days in—or maybe you've been doing it in hotel rooms on the trip (to the amazement of any maid who wanders in to change the sheets). My Uncle Stephen was visiting his brother Bill in Pleasantville, N.Y., once, and was lying on top of the living-room bookshelves, cleaning the clerestory windows, when a visitor arrived on some business or other. Stephen lay there, just below the ceiling, leaning on an arm and smiling down at the visitor. The visitor looked up at him, but said nothing. Bill also said nothing. Business was transacted and the visitor left, with no explanation of the strange sight he had just witnessed.

I can't claim to be a serious student of Zen, but it does seem to me you have one of the main points in "not being run around by thoughts, emotions, and physical energy." I love someone's comment: "I'm an old man and have had many troubles, most of which never happened." I have to slow my own mind down, or it runs away with me, to places I don't necessarily want to go right now. Here I should have your stamp: ☛**LAUGH AT IT**☚ Can't do stamps, but the computer has some fun things.

🌴 After quite a bit of time had passed . . . .

The drafts you sent of the Declaration of Independence are certainly amazing and priceless things. So fragile. I think it's time for me to dig into my typography files, including the materials for a "winter term" course in typography that I taught in the early '80s. I'll send you the first handout, about ancient scripts. (I could send a book on how to operate a Linotype machine, but this would probably be of limited utility.) Anyway, Ms. Dianne and Ms. Anne . . . if you decide to sign up for the class, I can send some more things, like the Gettysburg Address in Chinese. But only "if." I know you students have a lot to do, what with field trips to museums 🖼, sun-bathing on the beach 🏊, and reading 📖 . And of course standing on chairs.

You've mentioned from time to time the difficulties of getting under way with a piece of writing. Your comment—"you just have to start"—is better than any advice I could give. It's the Zen approach, isn't it?—

"Just cook." Just do it, without too much thinking about it and without worry about whether it will be any good or whether anyone else will care about it.

I was held back from writing for a long time because of people who told me that, if you didn't get it published and make money, the writing obviously wasn't any good. I eventually figured out this was bad advice, and that if I wanted to write I should just do it.

It's interesting—I have a close writing friend who has been a great help, and we exchange a lot of stuff. Her first reaction to something she likes is often, "Oh, you've got to send this out." Good advice and I do sometimes, but only if I feel like it. I've been able to use print-on-demand publishing to advantage, keeping the cost down by doing my own editing and formatting. That gets enough copies into print for friends, relatives, and a few other brave souls. I always figure that 100 years from now I'll have about as many books on library shelves as Tom Clancy.

And who knows what will last? At his death, the T'ang Dynasty poet Chia Tao had a wife, a donkey, and a zither—but he's still in print after a thousand years.

Karen and I are looking forward to our European trip Sept. 5-22. We'll see the Lipizzaner horses in Vienna, drink beer in Munich, and visit friends from Army days in Bavaria. There are a few projects before we go. I'm writing a grant proposal for the college here, to equip a "smart" classroom. Now I just have to find out what a smart classroom is. One with smart students? Does Anne have a smart classroom?

P.S. Make me a little stamp sometime that says **Just Cook**.

To Bill

HELLO, BILL

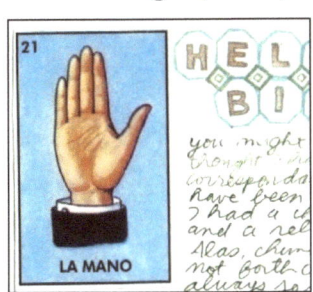

You might perhaps have thought I had abandoned our correspondence but no, I just have been waiting until I had a chunk of time and a relaxed mood. Alas, chunks of time are not forthcoming. There are always so many things I want to or have to do so I have decided to forge ahead with this rather shaky enterprise.

David and I are taking a trip-vacation-bonding time, leaving on the 22nd. Somehow we have ended with 10 days, 3 in Stockholm, 3 in Copenhagen, and 3 in Reykjavik because we are flying Icelandair which my son Nicholas advised has good fares.

We also have been moving our house all around, switching our living room to the sunporch, the bedroom to David's office, his office to a bedroom, and the living room to a sewing room. On top of that, some friends who we don't actually know well are moving in with us temporarily (but we don't know if that's 2 weeks or 2 months) while their house is being renovated. They are coming by later this weekend to decide which room they would like to use and we will move a bed. This is the world here just now (setting the background).

As I go along I will glue in things that I have here in a basket.

Yesterday Anne and I went to the beach in the late afternoon. The tide was high and the waves were unusually big. We had brought our beach chairs and sat there enjoying the salt smell and the booming sound of the waves as they crashed and the hiss as the water receded. Suddenly a bigger

wave approached and we were wet. Our clothes, my purse and all the stuff in my wallet. So I have just reloaded my license, my library card, and my slightly damp money. I can't wait until Anne gets back from school so we can go back and see how the ocean is today.

I have been extreme absorbed in my doll making. They are not exactly "dolls" per se but I am used to calling them that. They have gotten bigger and bigger so that now with their long legs they are as tall or taller than I am. Here are photos of a few of them. though actually not the most recent ones,

since I have 5 or six I am working on at once and they are all missing one piece or another—often lips which seem to be always a last-minute part. This one is made out of a mink stole of Marie's.

It had kind of a long face and it reminds me of you, Bill, at least a little so that's who I think of him as—BILL. I don't tend to name them but Anne likes to name things and she has names for them all. I just made my first one with genitals not exactly on purpose. I had some old thread that was breaking and David unwound it off the spool so it looked like a pile of pubic hair.

The doll I was working on was wearing a skirt, so I did go ahead and create her some private parts—then I took her to the shopping center to get some underpants. I sure got some odd looks carting her around the store. She has a pocket in her skirt so I think I'm going to make her a little photo album of her "friends" to go in the pocket.

Next week is the big shopping trip for sewing. Twice a year a church in Marblehead has a wonderful rummage sale. At the end, for $5 you can fill a garbage bag with whatever is left. I choose coats just for their

buttons and all sorts of clothing for the cloth. Sometimes when I am unpacking I find that I have brought home something someone can actually wear. Jeez, I keep noticing how poorly I write—I mean the actual forming of the letters. I hope you can read this all right.

After that last bit we began moving furniture around, one bed up, another down. But we couldn't get the queen box spring up the stairs. Someone said you can cut it and fold it, so I got out my little electric saw and in no time zip zip—cut, folded, and up the stairs. It was such fun to just do it and have it work out.

Then we went over to the folk-music venue where we have been volunteering now for a number of years. Tonight there was a Minnesota couple, Neal and Leandra. One song they sang had lyrics about how it doesn't matter if you live or die, soar or sink—as long as you love. Then Neal made some comment about sappy people and they proceeded to sing a song to God: "You resurrected Jesus & Lazarus, maybe you can resurrect our love." And now it is 10:45 p.m. Time for bed & to finish tomorrow. GOOD NIGHT—

MONDAY—GOOD MORNING. Yes, Sunday passed with nary a time at the desk.

We have a large collection of old books and magazines that we cut up for collage. Those could use weeding out, but in some ways they are hard to part with. I get used to looking at certain images and these cut-up pages are like old friends, friends who sacrifice for ART. I used to feel terrible about cutting up old books until another collage artist said to me, "What better use

for old books that to make art?"

All it took was writing about collage books for me to start rifling through them looking for images to combine. Sometimes the images call out to me—"Cut me out, play with me." This man with the newspaper was chasing a naughty goat in a 60s reading book. I have no goats but do get upset with where my mind goes. We did finish our 60 days of standing on chairs while on the trip and no one walked in on us, because we always put the "Do not disturb" sign on the door.

A beach picture is enclosed. This was in Kansas on one of those very hot days and a big Kansas sky. As we floated in the water, I saw a snake swim past. A first for me.

It's a beautiful sunny day today with a light breeze jiggling the autumn leaves so they look particularly radiant—time to take a shower and get dressed and go out & see the world. Bye for now, Dianne.

To Dianne

Dear Dianne,

THIS IS NOT A LETTER.

What this actually is is a gallery of pictures, which I shot in the Vienna Clock Museum with you and Anne in mind. This was an odd place, tucked down a side street near our hotel. We were the only ones there when we arrived, and the desk clerk urged us to use our camera.

The room with the marquetry clocks was especially—I almost said striking, and that would have been appropriate because all the clocks were wound and whispering to each other, with an occasional chime. The sound changed as one walked around the room, with new voices coming in as old ones faded. I could have stayed there a long time, but some other tourists arrived and we moved on.

Hope you enjoy the pictures. There will be a letter along with other trip tidbits.

To Dianne

One of the nice things about this correspondence is the absence of time pressure, or of any definite schedule. If the interval is stretching out too much, I can always send a card (yes, I'm still alive!), and then the right time eventually comes around for a letter. I've noticed a strange and somewhat disconcerting thing about age—people get concerned if they don't hear from you regularly, and begin fearing that you're sick, dead, or have lost your mind. Maybe you could make me a stamp with checkboxes:

Reasons for slow answer to your letter:
☐ **Sick**
☐ **Senile**
☐ **Dead**
☐ **Usual procrastination**

If it will not make you self-conscious (or even if it will, since I've already started), I'll tell you what goes on when an illustrated letter arrives. When yrs of Oct. 13 reached me, I carefully peeled off the tape-measure bits, not wanting to destroy any part of a work of art. I stuck some of the tape bits to the wall over my desk, where they stayed for a while until Karen asked, "Why do you have pieces of tape measure stuck over your desk?" They've now come down, but some sticky bits still adhere to the letter itself.

I read the letters right away, of course,  admiring not only the visual surprises, but also the interesting written content (and by the way your handwriting is perfectly legible). Then at some point I go back and really READ, and LOOK, and TAKE NOTES! Yes, notes, because the things that you write always startle a covey of thoughts, some of them high elliptical. Why, for instance, does the leaf print in your letter make me think of Ames, Iowa? This is actually easy, because when I was 12, I went with Jack for the summer to Iowa State where he was

working on his master's degree. And I collected leaves all over the ISU campus, and learned to make prints of them, with a crayon.

It's time for this letter to get organized. Let's try subject headings for a while.

Cutting up books: There was a little show several years ago at the John Herron Art Institute in Indianapolis by an artist who had done all sorts of horrible things to books—wrapped them in chains, soaked them in acid baths. The moral: it's okay to torture and even destroy books in the interest of art.

Vacations: What really came out of our Austria/Germany trip was a lesson in adaptation. Karen had just gotten over sciatica, and we walked too much getting to our Munich hotel, where our room turned out to be a fourth-floor walkup. That could have been a disaster, but WACW—With Age Comes Wisdom. The hotel was helpful and got us into a lower room. I went out and bought food so we could eat in the room the first night. Next day we sat around in the beer garden of the nearby farmers' market, reading the papers, drinking coffee, people-watching. We walked in easy stages, resting Karen's gimpy leg often. We had a lot of fun, saw a lot, didn't let somewhat limited mobility faze us. A few years ago, it all would have been irritating and annoying, a vacation spoiled. But WACW.

The Sealed Enclosure: This essay is a good-news medical story, about my really quite mild encounter with breathing problems. Since it was written, the doctor has sent me to "pulmonary rehab," which is really just exercise and education. It's supposed to last until Christmas, but they're about to toss me out—I'm making too rapid progress toward the goals!

Writing: You have an unusual gift, in your ability to write of life as you encounter it, with clear perception and your own voice. So just cook! It's always a matter of "I write to find out what I'm going to say." And there are even ways now to publish cheaply in small editions, and avoid agents and the whole squander of energy "in courting that world," as you once expressed it. This also frees one of some ego involvement.

Someone sent me a story last week about a young guy who's struck it rich with his first book, on a flashy/trashy historical subject. The agents/publishers swarmed him, and he thinks it's always going to be like this. And maybe it will—I'd love to sell a million copies, too. But there's a waste of spirit in focusing on that, I think. Just cook.

This 'n' that: Lots of little things in your letter that could inspire essays. On the beach—you were in a tsunami and didn't know it. And the lake/snake in Kansas. Wouldn't "Swimming Through Kansas" be a fine title? The dolls: They're remarkable and I see the resemblance in "Bill."

This could go on . . . and on. One thing leads to another. Bad mind, whap, whap. Gotta go.

 *To Bill*

A couple of days ago we took a walk on the beach and I noticed a snail moving along—well actually I noticed his trail. So I made a mark with my finger in the sand and when we had walked to the end of the beach and were coming back we could see that he was really moving along.

Thank you so much for the *Rain* book. I am a slow reader these days—I keep checking things out of the library and then returning them half read. But your book is one I can pick up here and there easily. I love it and I love you and I will write more completely before long.

Dear Bill,
a couple of
days ago we
took a walk
on the beach
and I noticed
a snail moving
along—well
actually I
noticed his
trail, so I made
a mark with
my finger in
the sand and
when we had

walked to the end of the beach and were coming back we could see
that he was really moving along.

We loved the pictures of all those clocks in Vienna,
and your description of them whispering & chiming.

thank you so THIS IS NOT A LETTER
much for the Fine Smirr of Rain. Reading it makes
me feel as if I am sitting with you as you smoothly

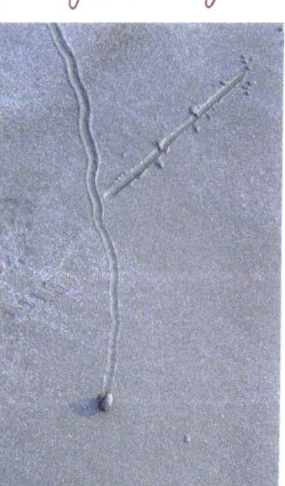

move from comments
about the science and
history to the poetry
of the thing. I am
a slow reader
these days—I keep
checking things out of
the library and then
returning them half
read. But your book
is one I can pick up
here and there easily.
I love it and I love
you and I will
write more completely before too
long, Dianne

Wednesday NOV 29 2006

28

DECEMBER
20

To Bill

It's only a week until Anne & I head to Dubai, to visit Nicholas and his family, and there is a lot in between but I really wanted to write to you before I leave. I didn't know quite how to start this so I began with a self-portrait—me in a mirror. When in doubt I often just draw myself. I'm available, I don't have to tell myself not to fidget and I don't mind if the drawing has little resemblance to me. I do notice more wrinkles and blemishes all the time. But I guess that's the way it's supposed to be.

The drawing is made with walnut ink using a stick as a pen, a technique I was advised to use when I was about 14 years old and had a bouncy ponytail. I took lessons from an artist named John Laurent at Perkins Cove in Ogunquit, Maine.

We had a nice visit with Colin in NYC last weekend. Peter had just finished classes and was staying with his high school buddy Ilya so we got to order lots of different Chinese dishes. Colin gave me a great print of a dog which I love. [Photo of Colin, Dianne, Ilya, Peter, and David] Oh oh. Time for a new ink cartridge in my photo printer.

[Dec. 22] Here it is another day, mostly shopping for the roast (we are having 16 for Christmas) and some roses and cat food to keep the felines happy while Anne and I are in Dubai with the sand and the camels and my little girls.

I loved hearing about how lovingly you

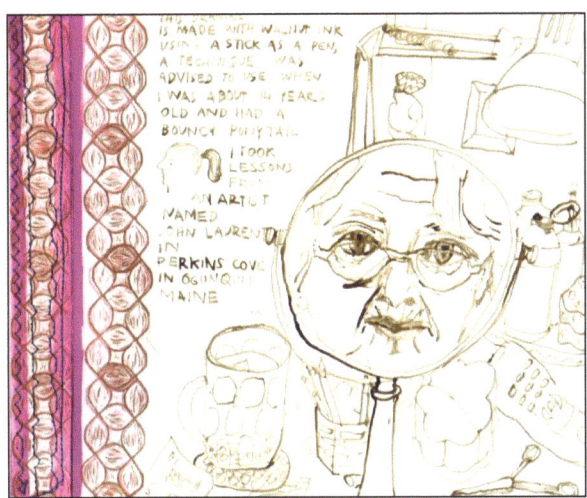

⬆ **Colin, Dianne, Ilya, Peter, David**

receive my letters and how you use them to bounce your memories off of. Sometimes it's hard for me to remember that you were a little boy and Jack was the Dad. I knew Jack for a long time before I met you. He must have been in his 60s then—it was old to me at the time, even though now I am 60. And by the time I really met you, you were in your 60s. This age thing is such an odd one, I can't quite get my mind around it. My parents were both in their 50s when they died but THEY WERE THE ADULTS. I guess my kids and grandkids think of me as the grown-up but I'm just me. Or maybe they think I am an immature adult. When I asked Nicholas what we should wear in Dubai, the one answer that came back was BRAS. I never liked Rodney Dangerfield but I would like some RESPECT.

About cutting up books: I took a three-week class on bookmaking some years ago at Haystack, a crafts school in far northeast Maine. The teacher carved hollows in books, stuck pins in them, and folded them. At the same time he was quite in love with books. I have trouble hurting books still. We eat on the way to New York at a restaurant that gives each patron three books with their meal. One I got last week was IT'S FUN TO MAKE IT YOURSELF—I liked the old-fashioned pictures of people working. One reminded me of Jack. I've been thinking of him lately and missing him. He was such a charmer for me. And I start looking at these unwanted cast-off books and I see this could really be useful. And I remind myself I got it for collage. I'm not a furniture person. That's a different kind of patience.

[Dec. 26] Hello again. It's late afternoon

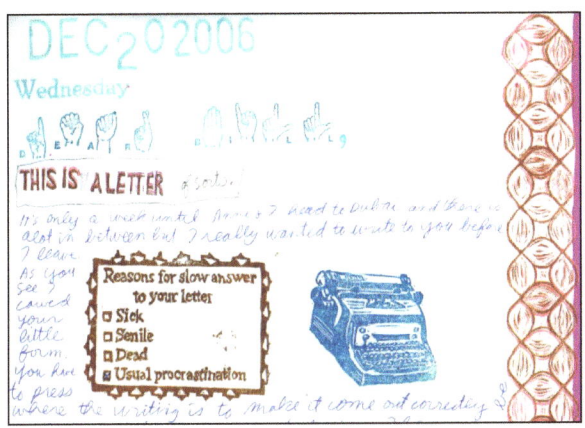

and I just returned from the post office to mail some bills. Some things are taken automatically but I still like to write the checks and put the stamps on the envelopes. I feel like a holdout, that the young ones will eventually not even know what a checkbook is.

We got through Christmas eve with my son, daughter-in-law, 5-year-old grandson and me, David, Peter, and my first husband and his wife. Luckily we are all OK with each

other. We talk about the kids, the grandkids, politics. Yesterday we had 16 guests. We ate, talked,

and ate some more. There is a certain amount of rearranging the house for a big group and by the time all the tables and chairs were back where they belonged I was sore all over and fell into bed moaning with exhaustion. Today has been tying up loose ends—cooking soup and chili for David and Peter to eat while we are in Dubai.

About your medical story, I think, "Oh Bill, breathing difficulties must be so scary" and "You better stick around so we can keep writing to each other."

And the roomers: Our friends found someone else who offered them a whole apartment and they wisely accepted that offer.

The "association wheel" [next page]: I love to make things like this as stimulants & playthings.

To Dianne

I was reading Gaston Bachelard today on the fear of snails, which he describes as an "insignificant" matter. After your inspired photographic observations on the speed of snails, I refuse to regard anything about them as insignificant.

But this is being coy, isn't it? Who, for Heaven's sake, is Gaston Bachelard, and why would anyone read his reflections on snails? It all goes back to the *Rain* book, and a copy I sent to a friend in England, Michael Snow, who replied that it reminded him of Bachelard's book, *The Poetics of Space*.

Well!!! What author wouldn't be "set up" over such a comment? Of course I trotted right over to the library to order the *Poetics*, and then hit the Internet for information about Bachelard, whom I had never heard of. Before his death in 1962, Wikipedia said, he was "an honorary professor at the Sorbonne and one of Europe's leading philosophers." Bachelard established his reputation as a philosopher of science, but then apparently fell among Jungians and poets, who convinced him that the only true reality was the imagination (I'm oversimplifying and no doubt

distorting). On the first run-through, I found his book pretty knotty, as well as vaguely irritating and tinged with sentimentality. Its thesis—again, much too simply—was that the poetic imagination is shaped by the spaces "inhabited" by poets, especially the ones in which they lived as children. There was a lot of ruminating, in a Victorian way, on memories of "the old home." Oh dear, I thought—another potty retired professor. I wonder if Michael is sending me a message?

But once you've been compared to "one of Europe's leading philosophers," you don't give up easily, so I began reading the book through again, taking notes this time.

And getting more and more intrigued by Bachelard's comments on the significance to the imagination of cellars and attics, wardrobes, locked caskets, nests, shells, corners of refuge, and solitary lights glowing from distant hermit huts. Something also chimed with the Zen I've been reading and descriptions of the huts of Chinese hermits, with brushwood doors. (I'm not sure what a brushwood door is, but every hermit hut seems to have one.) So the upshot is that I've decided to follow Michael's advice and just enjoy Bachelard's flights of fancy.

And now I think I'll have a scotch and go to bed. Tomorrow, Zen.

[Tomorrow, 1/4/2007] I'm afraid that under the anticipatory influence of scotch, I overpromised. It's difficult to write about

Zen without running counter to its spirit—but since you once stood on a chair for 60 days in a row, you will at least be a sympathetic audience.

We've talked about the Zen master Shunryu Suzuki, and one thing he insists on is the importance of *zazen*, or Zen sitting. I started this with some regularity a few months ago—just sitting, counting breaths, letting the mind clear. I wasn't very good at it, and Suzuki wasn't very specific about procedures, how long to sit, whether to close your eyes or not. For all I know you may be a Zen student of long standing, and smiling right now about my baby steps. I hope you're smiling.

Anyway, I dropped the practice for a while and then read some other descriptions that clarified things a little. So I'm now back sitting each morning, sometime between 4 and 8.

I've observed a few things. Apparently some beginners have problems keeping their attention on breathing, even to the count of ten. This was not my problem. In the beginning, I was counting to two or three hundred—but I'm good at multi-tasking, so one part of my mind was keeping count while another was flitting around the universe. And of course I was very proud of

> Before
> studying
> ZEN,
> men are men
> and mountains
> are mountains
>
> While
> studying
> ZEN,
> things
> become
> confused
>
> After
> studying
> ZEN,
> men are men
> and mountains
> are mountains

being able to do this. Bad mind, whap, whap. Now it's enough to do tens, and the focus is better. I keep reading Suzuki, who seemed very difficult at first, then too simple, and now difficult again. It reminds me of a piece of printing done by a friend of my Uncle Stephen's—a quotation from another Suzuki, Daisetz, who did much to popularize Zen in the '50s and '60s. It's hanging near me, and looks like the enclosed picture (which is how my Uncle Stephen's friend, John McLaughlin, set it up for his Piccolo Press).

Had a nice laid-back Christmas here. Colin came from New York, and also Dave, his wife Connie, and our granddaughter Rebecca. Grandpa and Rebecca have a big cookie-baking thing on, and we baked a different variety for four consecutive days. We began doing this when Rebecca was about three—our first effort was a batch of sugar cookies in the shape of the numerals

she was learning. "Take one to your Daddy," I said, and she carefully sought out a numeral 1 and went off with it, an early encounter with linguistic ambiguity.

To Bill

The card shows the Gold Souk. We haven't actually bought much but walking in the souks is wonderful, especially the spice stalls with all the smells and unusual whole spices that I have never seen before. Nicholas and his wife Laurence have treated us like royalty—we are the first family to come & visit—so we have taken camel rides in the desert, visited the ski slope in the mall, gone to the Sultanate of Oman for a few days, where we spent a day on a dhow, swimming, seeing dolphins, and enjoying the contrast of water and mountain.

To Dianne

THAT'S A SOUK? I always thought a souk was a dim and dusty (and, yes, smelly) place with merchants sitting cross-legged and haggling. And sinister characters in the shadows, with knives. Obviously I read too many adventure yarns as a kid. BUT THIS LOOKS LIKE A MALL!

To Dianne

To begin a letter, it is necessary to begin.—"Wisdom of Dianne"

Okay. For starters, I've just heard the sound of a forehead being smacked all the way from Australia.

The technical editor on my current book project (he's in Australia) has been remarkably obtuse, and has been declining to review a chapter because he can't get the computer-coded project in it to work. The chapter author (who is getting pretty tired of this) suggested I ask him whether he had in fact "deployed" the encoded project, since without doing so of course it's not likely to work. I asked the tech editor this, delicately. Answer: "Gosh, I didn't think of deploying it!" (sound of forehead smack). So this gets me started. I've been re-reading your Dec. 20 letter, which leads to several thoughts. The first is that you have a wonderful facility for describing your daily routines and occupations in a way that engages this reader. Most correspondents can't do that or are self-conscious about it— "Oh, you don't want to read about my going to Wal-Mart and having a display of waffle irons fall on my foot." But that's exactly what I want to read about. And here on the second page of your letter, I find that you

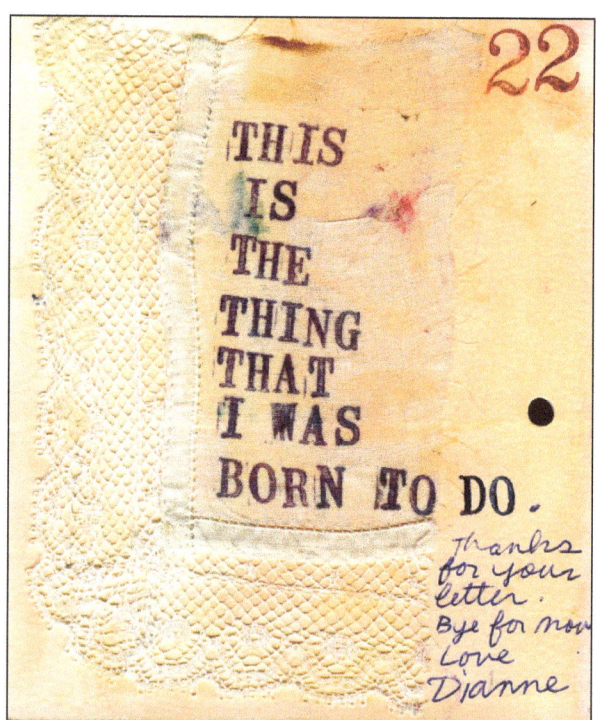

studied art at Perkins Cove in Ogunquit, Maine—and I'm wondering if you are a native Mainiac, and if Perkins Cove is anywhere near Beal's Island, which was the home of my old friend Velton Peabody, who (when he wanted to be totally incomprehensible) would lapse into Beal's Island dialect, and who had an uncle, Mariner Peabody, which I think is the greatest Downeast name ever. So there. You see why I don't move through letters very quickly.

Since you've written about your routines, here are some of ours. We're early risers usually—"First man up makes the coffee," Karen says. She heads for the computer to check the weather in the cities where we have children, and then drops in on a British news wire to see what crazy things our Limey friends are doing. There's always something—recently it was a man ticketed for having a horse in his car. Meanwhile, I have gone off upstairs to do *zazen* for half an hour—counting breaths, letting the mind go blank. Sometimes Batoo the cat sits with me—he's a much better Zennist than I am. When I began doing this, I warned Karen not to be alarmed "if you see me sitting and staring into space—it will just be Zen meditation." "How will I tell it from

the other times?" she said. (I found out recently that she hates it when I tell these stories on her—"People will think I'm some kind of harridan." So listen up, please. Karen is not a harridan.)

Now I have just re-read the "ploughed ground" page of your letter, with all the wavy lines. Yes, that was hard going, but interesting to someone who's studied typography. Much of the technical part of reading has to do with getting back to the start of the next line—and the wavy lines absolutely destroy this! But fun anyway. Parenthetically, I prefer the spelling "plough" to "plow," because it looks more like ploughed ground, with clods sticking up and down.

A little follow on my recent "don't worry about my health" note. Saw my super-expert doctor again on Tuesday, and he says I'm doing fine, don't come back for six months. I quizzed him about "alveoli," those little breath sacs of which we all carry around about 300 million in our lungs. I wanted him to tell me their average diameter, but he said, "You're thinking like an engineer, and we're physicians. Everybody's alveoli are different. Let's just say they're really tiny."

Have just started a curious book (by Max Picard) called *The World of Silence*, which presents silence as the necessary background for significant speech. And makes a point of how the overwhelming noise around us damages both language and silence. (And he was writing in the 1950s!).

Well, these are certainly crazy times we live in. What monumental silliness in Boston, with the "explosive devices" that turned out to be advertising messages. Leave it to the ad industry to figure out how to commercialize terrorism. And leave it to almost any politician to go nuts, over almost anything. A sober friend in California suggests the culture is about where Germany was in the 1930s, with everything sensible crumbling. But then we old codgers have always thought that, haven't we? Live your life the best you can. Breathe in, breathe out.

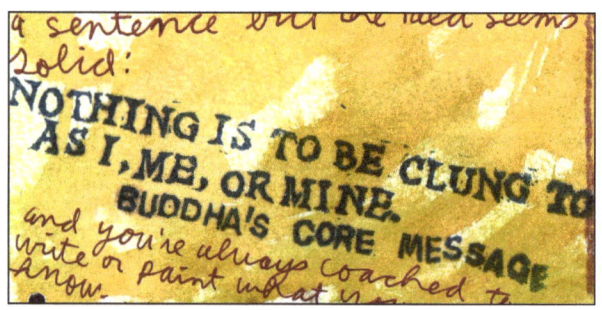

 *To Bill*

I was painting some polkadots on a chair yesterday and decided to play with some bits of leftover paint to write you a note. But just now I looked and see that I have a REAL letter to respond to (the one about snails & Zen) but this is not a REAL LETTER. I think of this as INTERIM MAIL—just a note to say yes, I think of you but no I'm not ready to write a real letter.

 *To Bill*

Thank you so much for sending *Zen Mind, Beginner's Mind,* and your writing about meditation experiences. I have started a real letter today. (I folded the paper, so in a week or so it will be on its way to you.)

 *To Bill*

The artwork has been ready to go on this for a while. I've been thinking that I would "get myself together" before I started writing, but that hasn't happened so

now I am hoping that I will "get myself together" by writing.

Last week we went down to New Haven to hear an artist we admire—Chuck Close—talk about art & museums. He had some kind of a spinal cord thing 10 years ago (or 20) and so he's in a wheelchair. He gestured a lot while he was talking but his

on a desert island would
cut his hand so he could draw with blood
on a leaf. He said his work was about
having an audience I found that upsetting and after
the talk I went up and asked him about it and he compared creating

hands are messed up and in the photos I've seen of him at work he has his paintbrush strapped onto his hands. It's kind of how I think of him—physically messed up and yet going on making great big paintings that are very much his own style.

So in his talking he said that he wasn't the kind of artist who, if he found himself stranded on a desert island, would cut his hand so he could draw with blood on a leaf. He said his work was about having an audience. I found that upsetting, and after the talk I went up and asked him about it and he compared creating art for oneself to masturbating. I asked "what about all the artists who aren't big successes," and he said, "They keep hoping." And as I write this I think of you and the way you get your books published so they can get out in the world. I haven't figured out how to get my stuff in the world except by making things for people or having them around and bringing the world in. Maybe part of why I have so much company is to justify and share the blessings here. Food as a metaphor for love.

Well, this sheet is getting pretty much

used up and so I will find another piece of paper and write on it first and then decorate it. Maybe I will mail them separately.

PART 2

ooh now what? This page sure looks big.

okay, now I've made a pencil circle to write inside of, oh oh ending a sentence with a preposition. I see it coming, I am horrified, and I do it anyhow.

I have reread your last 2 letters, the one about Zen and an earlier one from December, that you begin with the quote from Bachelard about snails and then the discussion of his *Poetics of Space*! I stop to hear these ideas resonating in me and stare out at the blue sky.

When you describe Bachelard's stress on childhood I think of a passage in Rainier Maria Rilke's *Letters to a Young Artist* where he speaks of childhood as the treasure house to write from and also about locked rooms with no answers and about living with them until someday a key is given. Years ago, our writers' group did a workshop where part of the meditation was to see our bodies and minds as houses. I remember going exploring in the attic and all the wonderful forgotten treasures there. I often have a dream that there is another house connected to the one we have and that I had forgotten it was there. This great abundance right through a little door. It always seems to me a hopeful happy dream—there is so much more that belongs to me.

There is another world, but it is in this one— Paul Eluard

No, I am not a native Mainiac, but I did spend every summer in Ogunquit which is about an hour south of Beal's Island—I think this is up near Bowdoin College where they are renovating their excellent small art museum. Mariner Peabody was a lobsterman, wasn't he? He had to be on a little boat pulling up traps and talking to the shellfish.

CONTINUED

This is fun. I went downstairs and scored this sheet on the big table and I am leaving room to "decorate" and it's like getting to have dessert later. Usually I decorate first and then write.

Again, thanks for the Zen book. Since the early 1970s I have been reading books about Zen. In the mid-70s my old husband and I got involved in a mystical school called ARICA. There was lots of meditation involved but with chanting and physical activity and staring at dots in the middle of esoteric images. David was there in that period; we all lived in group houses doing "spiritual work" together. Later we all got involved with a new teacher who espoused a different kind of meditation. This teacher also said that when he spoke he would take us with him "soul traveling" to higher realms. Soul traveling looked a lot like sleep to me but we were devotees and this wasn't something one was supposed to say. I've since become a serious skeptic of "teachings," but Zen continues to appeal to me.

The ink drawings on this page are from the middle of the night on Wednesday. It's very rare for me to be unable to sleep and I do like being up at night, not having anyone's needs pressing on me. I drew, and read a novel by Wallace Stegner, called *Crossing to Safety*. It's lovely to read an old-fashioned, straightforward novel about regular people. The book that I read before this was Dave Eggers' *What Is the What*, a novel form but mostly an autobiography of

There is another world,
but it is in this one.
Paul Eluard

one of the lost boys from Sudan. The writing was fine but the story was so sad and upsetting that I could only bear a little bit at a time.

Last night David and Peter went out, so Anne and I ate grilled cheese sandwiches and discussed life: What are we supposed to do here, what matters; and from that the question of how we got here and where are we going. I've been around enough Buddhism and new age thinking to have certain belief systems down but that's all they are—someone's ideas about it all. I look up and see the ocean and the shore through the tangle of branches in front of the window.

 *To Dianne*

This is just a quick note to let you know that the bee-yoo-ti-ful BIG letters have both arrived and are being savored. More on them later, but I'm moved to comment on Chuck Close's observations about solitary artists.

It's not so much that I think he's wrong, as I do that he misses the mark somehow. His comments (to me) tell

something about his own ideas of success—which are not necessarily bad ideas, just limited.

Most of us have some idea of audience, and even like the idea that we're not creating just for our own amusement. You certainly have an audience among family and friends. Choosing not to push beyond that is simply a decision, and should be respected, I think. His remark about minor artists ("They keep hoping") implies that without acceptance and even applause, there's no point in creating something. And the remark also implies that the hope of a reaction is all that keeps an artist going.

Strange, that's not my experience at all. When I began writing poetry, it was a sudden breaking in of something. I knew I wasn't very good at the technical part of it, so I began to work very hard in order not to wreck whatever was coming in—or to shut that little door in my house through which it was coming.

Oh, I wasn't oblivious to the idea of audience, but it was not a very big concern. Eventually, I did start submitting to litmags, but partly to get feedback from editors so I could spot my mistakes and quit making them. But I figured out that editors weren't infallible either—I remember getting a rather curt rejection of a poem about Venice, in which the editor observed that I had misppelled [ha!] the name of the Church of the Gesuati—it should have been Gesuiti, she wrote. Well, I was *not* wrong. Venice has two churches, one with each spelling. I even have a floor plan, see? ⇨ I wrote back nicely and pointed out the editor's error—and the poem was accepted. This was nice, but I think it was out of editorial embarrassment. So much for objectivity.

Well, that's enough. Many artists feel like Close, I'm sure, especially if they're trying to make a living at their art—which is a fine and worthwhile thing to do. But there are other artists and other views—the Creative Angel pops in on all sorts of people and should be welcomed happily. If there's an audience, fine. If there's not, that's fine, too.

Gesuati
Floor pattern Mass
Sketched during
May 26, 1974

⇧ **Floor pattern, Church of the Gesuati**

 **MARCH 18**   *To Bill*

Thanks for your postcards. It is always nice to get something in the mail that is not a bill or a credit card offer.

Our houseguests have left and we are enjoying the sunporch now that it is ours again. On Friday night we had a snowstorm and we read, sewed, ate and slept on the sunporch to be surrounded by all the windows (on three sides). It was like being in the snow but warm.

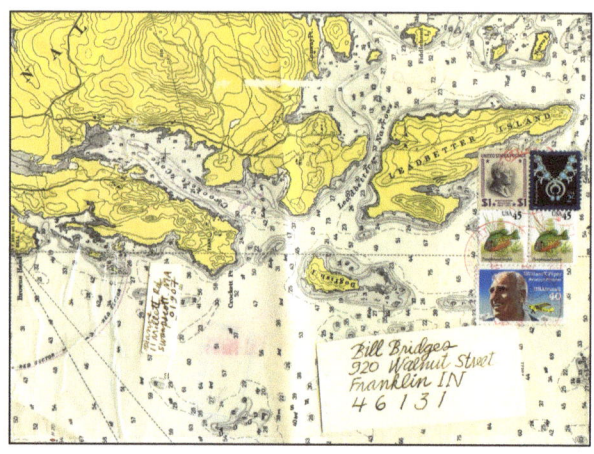

To Bill

We bought a bag of these maps for $1 at a yard sale but I still feel guilty using them not as maps.

To Dianne

About 25 years ago, as a new journalism department chair at the college, I got well "roasted" by students at the annual J-picnic. After making fun of all my other peculiarities, they came to the pièce de résistance. "And besides all that," the ringleader said, his voice dropping to a hiss, **"he still uses carbon paper!"**

I did and I do. It gets harder to find with the years, but I keep a good stash and use it whenever, as now, I'm typing on my Uncle Bill's 1922 Remington. The Rem is a relief from computers and also forces me to organize my thoughts if I don't want the letter to be a mess of strikeovers. (There will be some, I'm sure.)

Your letters are a joy to re-read. This morning I'm looking at the smaller images around the edges of the big Jackson Pollock-style paintings. Your rubber stamps of typewriters remind me that there's a room in an art museum in Hamburg with about three dozen typewriters fastened upside-down to the ceiling. And I like the little wire-haired dogs that pop up in a couple of places. And the reclining Buddha, which reminds me how much I'm enjoying the copy you sent of *Zen Flesh, Zen Bones*. Some of the stories are staples of Zen writing, but no less enjoyable for that.

I'm trying to take seriously Shunryu Suzuki's advice not to take Zen too seriously. His light touch appeals to me—I find some Zen writers very **earnest** and too fixated on labels and mechanics. This morning I'd been sitting *zazen* only a few minutes when Karen called up, "Sausage is ready!" I had a moment of thinking, "Don't interrupt me," but that's entirely contrary to the spirit of Zen—so instead I went downstairs and had a good breakfast and chit-chat.

Suzuki would have approved, I think. He avoids more than most the plague of "teachings" you mention. I've acquired a real dislike over the years for theology, whether Old Testament or New Age. It's all people theorizing about things they know nothing about first-hand, and want others to accept on faith. I remember being turned off philosophy in college by Leibnitz and his theory of "windowless monads" (don't ask me to explain, I can't). But it struck me at that young age that L. was an immensely gifted and brilliant man spinning theories, the realities of which he had not a shred of evidence for.

I happily end that sentence with a preposition.

Interesting that you quote Rilke and Paul Eluard. Both are quoted extensively by Gaston Bachelard. Bachelard was also high on Max Picard and his book *The World of Silence*. I did a little rummaging in Picard, but there's a strain of windy German romanticism that I'm not quite in sympathy with.

A remark in your letter, about the guru's routine, resonated here: "It looked like sleep to me." Oh, wonderful! I broke out laughing.

I'm leaving for a while. Unlike the computer, with the Rem you can leave something up on the screen while doing something else.

——————————

EMPTY SPACE

——————————

Actually, I left for a couple of days, and it's now Easter night. Things got busy suddenly on the freelance editing and literary fronts. One of my tech-book authors had surgery, which sent deadlines into a tailspin. But everyone coped, the author is recovering, we're almost back on track. And her neurotic co-author, faced with a real problem, quit whining and rose to the occasion.

On the lit front, a friend who

AS SOON AS YOU HAVE MADE A THOUGHT, LAUGH AT IT. —LAO TSU

critiques my writing has gotten after me for overusing "a lot" and "lots of." In despair, I programmed the computer's auto-correct function to automatically replace the offending phrase with %*$X;&5$. Alas, the Rem cannot be so programmed.

I think I'll get *Crossing to Safety* by Stegner. This will be right after polishing off a little biography about an odd figure in 19th Century entertainment, Adah Isaacs Menken, who wrote pretty awful poetry and performed Tchaikovsky's "Mazeppa," in which she rode a horse nude on stage. Well, not really, she had a body stocking—but it was still pretty racy for the 19th Century.

Realize I'm dodging your thoughts on "what does art mean"—I think because it's a question only the artist can answer. You're moved to make the dolls, so what business is it of anyone's whether you try to sell them or not? I enjoyed so much seeing them around the house while I was there. Maybe you actually <u>are</u> running a gallery.

And now I think I'll take another break, because it's late and I want to address toasted-cheese sandwiches at length.

——————————————

*

EMPTY SPACE WITH STARS

*   *   * *
* *

——————————————

And so time passed. And now it's Thursday and . . . toasted cheese sandwiches. These are one of my few kitchen specialties, and I've developed a technique for them. Butter both the top and bottom, of course, to grease the skillet and produce a good crust.Then use **two** slices of Kraft American, sprinkled liberally with olive bits. Fry until brown, gooey, and delicious.

'How was your time on earth? What did you do there? How did it feel?'

I've been celebrating my 72nd birthday all week—a rolling celebration that has included phone calls from kids and a "party in a box" from granddaughter Rebecca—cookies, party hats, a noisemaker, and other knick-knacks. Fun!

What a grab-bag of a letter this is—much like my mind. You are not alone in concern over the whirl of thoughts.

Standing on chairs and various other meditations do help. But the mind is certainly busy, busy, and why not? There's a nice story in a book by an "insight" writer, Larry Rosenberg. He said he worked diligently at stopping his mind and finally told his master that he had succeeded in not thinking. To which the master exclaimed, "What's wrong with thinking?"

The book on Adah Isaacs Menken was a disappointment. Dull, plodding work by a young Ph.D who failed to rewrite her doctoral dissertation for a general audience. This was a subject difficult to be dull about, but she managed it. Sigh.

Your letters are never dull, and each one is like opening a Christmas present, except that I don't rip off the wrapping. I disassemble it instead. Next to me is a card with strips of blue tape from the last one, and also the squiggly pieces of blue-green bias tape. You may get this back sometime

as a collage—but not in this letter, which is already long enough.

Don't have an ocean outside my window, but a lilac is coming into bloom in the neighbor's yard, defying a very cold, wet spring.

 *To Bill*

Hello Bill. Thank you for the great big letter and all the thoughts and words. I am not quite ready to write a letter but I wanted you to know that yours arrived here

POLKA DOT·INTOXICATION

and is much appreciated.

We have had three spring days in a row and the trees are rushing to put out blossoms and people (me included) have rushed to the beach—afraid that spring is a mirage that will fade as quickly as it arrived. Maybe. Til later.

MAY 5

To Bill

Saturday night, 9:10 p.m., but it feels like 2 a.m.

I got these funny foldover notes, a pack of about 10 for a nickel at my favorite rummage sale today.

David said, "You could send a note to Bill on one of these." So I am.

I started a letter to you yesterday—no words yet but a little booklet form constructed. I figure I may get it in the mail in a week if things go well.

It seemed like this paper is so thin and fragile that pencil is the safest material to write with.

MAY 8

To Bill

I've been playing around with this for a few days and now I am almost ready to write. But I have a cold and I am kind of cranky so I will wait until tomorrow. Hopefully tomorrow.

[Thursday, May 10] Good morning Bill. One way I know that it is time to write a letter is that I begin writing it in my head. I have had the "Good morning Bill" going this morning so I will start even though "Good morning Bill" is all I've got.

Conserve la calma

A couple of years ago when Anne & I visited Mexico we saw these signs telling what to do in case of fire or earthquake and they all began with CONSERVE LA CALMA.

Tuesday MAY 8 2007

HELLO HELLO

I've been playing around with this for a few days and now I am almost ready to write

But I have a cold and I am kind of cranky so I will wait til tomorrow. Hopefully tomorrow...

Maybe I should get a tattoo of that. I got this one tattoo last fall of the words SACRED + ORDINARY wound around my wrist like a bracelet and I've been thinking about what else to get. The waitress, an older woman, at a local lunch place noticed my tattoo and said the only thing she would ever consider tattooing on herself was her grandchildren's names. I started thinking about that and I thought if I was going to have my grandchildren then I should have my children and what about my spouses and my brothers and my friends and I imagined how fun it would be to point out to people—"See Bill, there's your name over by my elbow." And the kids would love to see their names on me. It does seem a little excessive and weird. Maybe I should just make a list of all the people I know and love and put it up someplace. Maybe I will get a big canvas and paint the names. So that's one kind of place my mind has been lately. Tattoos.

It's another gorgeous day here and part of what I aim for each day is to be good . . . yesterday I put all the screens in on the sunporch since it is suddenly really spring here. Last year I only managed to put about half of them in so I am very pleased with myself. The first 45 minutes of putting them in was very frustrating. I always forget how you're supposed to line them up and I keep dropping them into the yard and also I knocked off the window shades 3 times and they would fall off and hit me in the nose. Finally I took the shades off before I put in the screens.

Last week I took some photos of some of the dolls but they are not so great. I got a big roll of white felt to use as a backdrop at last weekend's rummage sale and am thinking to set it up outside. This lady has safety pins as part of her "theme" and her teeth are little white shells from the beach in Oman.

Peter came home last Thursday and we go back again to Troy New York for his graduation Friday. He starts his job in NYC in July so he is in a dither. I swear when people come into this house they revert to younger more dependent ages. I've started waking up at night in a panic about what everyone needs and how can I help them. Other family news is that David's oldest grandson became a father yesterday. So I'm married to a Great Grandpa. OK. Enough. As you can see, family stuff is preoccupying me. My grandson Jacob turned 6 years old and last weekend was his—my son's in-laws, who we like a lot, were up from NJ for the big birthday party, which we all went to with 30 kids, and then we all had brunch the next day—all this includes an entourage of Jacob admirers—me, David, Anne, the

parents, the wife's parents and my ex-husband & his wife—who are nice and we all get along.

The wife, who was a prima ballerina and danced before the Shah and President Kennedy and Kings and Queens, has written a memoir, and I heard David telling them about your publishing experience. There was an article in the *New York Times* last weekend about how many books are written each year and how few make it into print. It was an unbelievably high number that never get printed.

I've always been a little nervous about Germany (as a Jew) but your description of the museum in Hamburg with typewriters on the ceiling is almost enough to make me want to go. Anne has been collecting typewriters for the last few years—not with any rhyme or reason—just if we see them at a yard sale for cheap we get them. In spite of this big house we don't exactly know where to put them. I had considered putting our globe collection on the ceiling.

I agree with your idea of taking seriously the advice not to take Zen too seriously. It probably applies to the whole show here. I pop into moments of recognition that I don't know much about what's happening here and a whole lot of what I think I know is sort of a shared idea about reality that may have nothing to do with what is actually real.

I've never heard of Leibnitz and his windowless monads. Is that really a word or did you mean nomads? I imagine people trudging from place to place, so sad because they have no windows to look out of.

Many of the phrases in your writing stir me up—you speak of windy German romanticism and I see the trees blowing in the world of silence. And the THINKERS. I can see them, bent a bit as they walk into the wind, their heads down, not really seeing as they focus inward thinking their deep silent ideas.

I liked your little story about Larry Rosenberg's trying to stop his mind and the master saying, "What's wrong with thinking?" It's seemed to me that the idea is to observe the thinking, to get enough height to get a sense of this scene and of one's mind, not to judge it or change it but to just observe it. Maybe that's it or maybe not. Sometimes I think I know something and then I realize that is bullshit.

Last week I took some photos of some of the dolls but they are not so great. I am thinking to make another try today. I got a big roll of white felt to use as a back drop at last weekend's rummage sale and I am thinking to set it up outside. This lady has safety pins as part of her [...] her eyes and teeth are little white shells from the bead in OMAN. I have never planted a garden. Well, I did try once but found I hated the feeling of dirt under my fingernails

Your description of the grilled cheese sounds so good. The olives are a new addition. Do you use green or black? And when is your birthday actually?

I have the door to the art room open and can hear the sound of saws from somewhere below, a house down the street. And I smelled David's aftershave as he left the bathroom a few minutes ago. While I was writing I heard the garbage men come and I was disappointed to not have a chance to look through our neighbor's trash. The house is on the market and they are cleaning out in a frenzy and I have found various old objects to use in my dolls.

Sorry this letter is so jumpy. But I think of you often and wish you a happy spring & early summer.

JUNE 17

To Dianne

I've been having trouble starting a letter, but now this one seems to be starting willy-nilly. I'm about to take off for a PR stint in Washington, D.C.—maybe I'll take this along with me aboard the laptop.

Think I'll write a little about art.

My daughter-in-law Amanda (Mike's wife) is a multi-talented craftsperson, who paints, weaves, spins, throws pots—i.e., she puts me to shame as a creative artist. She brought her spinning wheel along on a recent visit, and I managed to produce a "yarn baby"—a lumpy coil of wadded wool, all mine and testimony to my inability to keep the tension right and to "draft" the wool properly. (I have also done some weaving. See photo of rather raggedy piece

known around here as "Aztec Sunrise.")

Amanda also touted me on a little book called *Art & Fear*, by David Bayles and Ted Orland. You might enjoy reading it, although you already know most of what the authors have to say. Once in a while they make me laugh—as when they write about artists who try unsuccessfully to duplicate the achievement of past greats. They offer some "cowboy wisdom" about this: "When your horse dies, get off."

One of the things I enjoy about your letters is that you ask questions in a way that indicates you really want answers, and aren't just being polite. So quickly, here are some answers.

My birthday is April 10, 1935—the day on which the U.S. Patent Office was founded, some years earlier. (I believe a humorist once wrote a story about an English/Russian detective named Reginald Uspatoff.)

Yes, a tremendous amount of stuff gets written but never published (some of it mercifully). But anyone who really wants to see work in print can do it fairly cheaply through print-on-demand publishing. It may only sell three copies, but it's there, in print,

⇧ **"Aztec Sunrise"**

with a Library of Congress number! I use green olives (the sliced-up bits) on toasted cheese, but black would be just fine, I suppose.

Tattooing. I was in a museum once (have no idea where) that had wonderful photographs of tattooed people, some of them nearly bare with virtually every inch of skin embellished. It was beautiful, in a bizarre way.

Yes, it was monads, but thanks to you I now have an indelible mental image of a tribe of Windowless Nomads, trudging across Arabia Deserta and never seeing a thing from their hermetically sealed tents.

[June 28, Thursday] Well, I did get to Washington and wrote press releases for the American Baptist centennial, and this afternoon revisited the Phillips Collection, north of Dupont Circle. It's certainly worth a visit, if you and Anne haven't seen it. Lots of Pierre Bonnard, Picasso, Braque, and American impressionists. Renoir's "Luncheon of the Boating Party" is there. But I wanted mainly to revisit old friends from 1993, when I spent a summer as a "faculty intern" for the Washington bureau of Scripps Howard. The manager of my rooming house worked at the museum, and got me a pass by saying I was his father. So I spent a lot of time there.

To my surprise and joy I found most of my favorites still on the walls. A Richard Diebenkorn ("Girl With Plant") that knocks my socks off. All the Bonnards. A couple of pieces by Pierre Puvis de Chavannes,

including "Marseilles" which I described in 1993 as

> *endlessly mysterious. People in a boat (but who are those shadowy giant figures?) . An old Orthodox priest reading his Bible, the crewmen, the woman in yellow standing calmly against the rail, the man like a gladiator in the foreground.*

Have I learned anything in 14 years? I see now that some of the figures make a group, held together by the carpet on which they repose—the girl in yellow, the old priest (who perhaps is a rabbi), a child in a red smock, all tied in some way. The foreground figures seem less facilely Roman and more elemental—a very strange crew indeed for this peculiar boat.

Gosh, I want to meet you and Anne in Washington sometime and introduce you to all these folks. Here's a sketch of them.

NO MAN CAN PROVE UPON
AWAKENING THAT HE IS THE MAN
WHO HE THINKS WENT TO BED THE
NIGHT BEFORE, OR THAT ANYTHING
HE RECOLLECTS IS ANYTHING
OTHER THAN A CONVINCING DREAM
~R. BUCKMINSTER FULLER

To Bill

I have been glad for your mail but buried in this household. Today is my first day at my desk in about 7 weeks. Busy cooking, washing beach towels, playing at the beach, sweeping up sand, baking cookies & pies.

Now I am tired. Seventeen days until Anne and I go to Seattle.

Hope you enjoy the card with the quotation from Buckminster Fuller.

61

To Dianne

NOT REALLY A LETTER . . . Well, yes, maybe, sort of a not-quite-letter.

Dearest Dianne,

This probably won't get to you before you and Anne take off for Seattle. But if it should, let me recommend the Elliott Bay Bookstore in the old part of town, which has every sort of printed matter as well as a nice coffeeshop/snack bar.

I have been buried, too, but not in anything as fun as going to the beach or baking cookies. At the moment, I have three computer-tech books going, with authors spread from Carmel, Indiana, to Tehran. The Iranian is the easiest to work with—does what he's told, meets his deadlines. Allah be praised. The Carmel guy is a little snooty (sometimes spelled with one "o" and two "t"s).

Am about 20,000 words into a new book of my own, titled *Places & Stories*. These are assorted travel essays that I thought could just be shoveled into a book, but am finding must be "revisioned" and rewritten. A chapter on a 1959 visit to Chartres Cathedral required re-reading Henry Adams's *Mont St. Michel and Chartres*, the indispensable book on the subject. You mustn't confuse Henry Adams (as I often do) with Henry James, who wrote all the difficult novels, and about whom Clover, the wife of Henry ADAMS, once said, "Henry chaws more than he bites off."

Loved your card with the Bucky Fuller quote. Karen and I once dragged our 10-year-olds to hear him lecture in Louisville. Don't remember much about it though. Think we were probably distracted by keeping two boys in line—one of our misguided efforts to force-feed them culture.

Oops, this is in danger of becoming a letter, so I'll quit. Have a good time in Seattle, and tell me about it.

To Bill

DANGER, MAY BE BORING AND BADLY WRITTEN

I started this by cutting out the paper and punching holes and sewing it together. I addressed it and put some nice postage stamps on the front and then I decorated the edges so I would know where to start

and stop when writing. Then I stepped on it and tore the binding. So throughout you will see little repairs. I hope you can see them as grit rather than sloppiness.

Anne and I are planning to visit Nick & his family in Dubai again at Christmas break and we are all planning on going to southern India for about a week. Nick called

today to tell me that one of his clients is AIR ARABIA and if we give them the dates and some things we'd like to see, they will make all the arrangements. I have never been to India, so that's pretty exciting.

Your last letter did get to us before we left for Seattle. We did get to the Elliott Bay Bookstore. There are many bigger but none warmer or more friendly. All over the bookstore on the shelves they have little reviews of the books by various people who work in the store. It's really sweet—you can picture the kid with the piercings praising the latest hot graphic novel and see the guy with the beard talking about the hiking book.

Your book of *Places & Stories* sounds lovely. Travel is such a lovely way to spend time— all the worries are so immediate and the drudgery of life is back there at home.

[September 27] I noticed this morning that I had the wrong date for yesterday. It doesn't really matter—and yet. It's early afternoon and I have been mostly running around—either for real, physically—to the farmers' market, the grocery store, to do some laundry, or tidy up downstairs. And/or mentally. Anne and I have been standing. It used to be on a chair, but now we just stand for ten minutes. It's not much, but there I am, on the deck, staring out at the sky and my mind just comes and goes. It makes me sad to think how little I am really present in this life. I wish I could do it better.

I have been re-reading a book I like called *When Things Fall Apart* by Pema Chödrön, an American Buddhist nun. She talks a lot about LOVING KINDNESS TOWARD ONESELF. I like that idea but I was somehow brought up to disparage myself— assuming that self-deprecation was sort of meek or modest. NOT.

You sent an old postcard showing the temple in Kyoto with "nightingale floors."

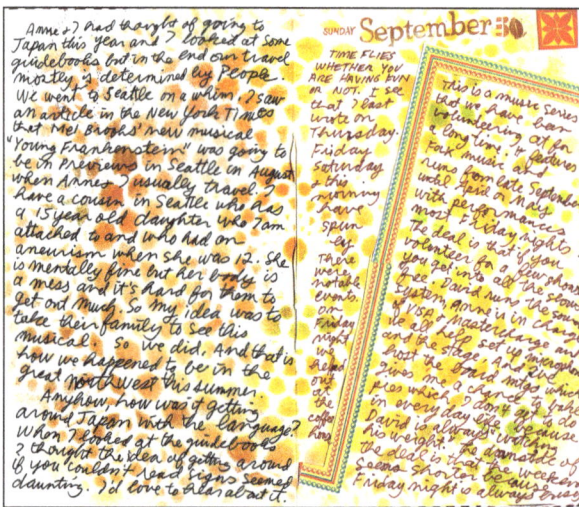

So if the floor squeaks when there is an assassin walking across it, does it squeak for other people as well? Years ago David was going to Asia quite often for Polaroid and I intended to go with him one time. Then all of a sudden it was over. He was retired. Done.

Anne & I had thought of going to Japan this year and I looked at some guidebooks, but in the end our travel is usually determined by people. We went to Seattle on a whim. I saw an article in the *New York Times* that Mel Brooks' new musical, "Young Frankenstein," was going to be in previews in Seattle in August when Anne and I usually travel. I have a cousin in Seattle who has a 15-year-old daughter who I am attached to,

and who had an aneurysm when she was 12. She is mentally fine but her body is a mess and it's hard for them to get out much. So my idea was to take the family to see this musical. So we did.

[September 30] TIME FLIES WHETHER YOU ARE HAVING FUN OR NOT. I see that I last wrote on Thursday. And now Friday, Saturday & this morning have spun by. There were notable events. On Friday night we helped out at the coffeehouse. This is a musical series that we have been volunteering at for a long time. David runs the sound system, Anne is in charge of Visa & Mastercharge, and we all help set up microphones and the stage. But this week I was really dreading going. We had been so busy and I wasn't crazy about the performer.

But I went. It was nice to see the other volunteers, and the singer, who I had not seen in two years, was wonderful. The coffeehouse has been going for 34 years or something, so often performers start coming when they are starting out and keep coming every two years for the rest of their careers—as they move up the ladder in their song-writing and delivery abilities, many of them get more & more popular, so we start

66

off paying them $50 and only a few people come to hear them, and eventually we're paying them $2,000 and they are filling the house.

I also took these photos on the beach Friday afternoon. I glued them into this letter yesterday and see now that they are upside down. Just the water on the sand. Whenever it is warm, we say, "Oh, it could be the last beach day," so we drag the chairs over and sit.

Saturday morning a church in the next town had its big annual rummage sale and we came home with many treasures. Over the years we have begun many collections: rulers and tape measures, playing cards, buttons, plates with scenes on them, etc., etc. Is there anything you like to collect that we can look for in our shopping adventures?

I have been continuing to read Pema Chödrön and in today's reading she talks

about impermanence as an essential part of life. That all changes—recognizing this is an essential part of her idea of a spiritual practice. So I made a carving this morning.

I've read that people don't get interested in being self-realized or finding higher consciousness until they are well fed and their lives are pretty easy. When couples are struggling to feed a family and keep themselves alive there isn't too much time for searching for meaning in their relationship.

Now I am back to your mail. I have spent some time at the Phillips. When my older son, Alexander, was in law school he broke his arm and I went down to help him when he came home from the hospital. It was one of the best trips ever. Alex was heavily medicated and mostly needed to sleep and he lived right there at Dupont Circle, so I spent a few days getting to know the Washington art museums.

ALL OF A SUDDEN I AM SICK OF MY VOICE. SICK OF MY LOUSY HANDWRITING. SICK OF MY STUPID LAME WRITING. THROW THIS OUT IF YOU WANT. DON'T READ IT.

...an essential part of life. That all changes, that recognizing it, the impermanence is an essential part of her idea of a spiritual practice. So I made this carving this morning.

RECOGNIZE IMPERMANENCE

TOO LATE. I'LL HAVE TO WRITE A WARNING IN THE FRONT. DANGER— MAY BE BORING AND BADLY WRITTEN.

Last year when we went to Dubai we stayed more than 2 weeks. At 10 days I  suddenly thought, "OH NO we are staying too long. They are sick of us. How could I ever have imagined it would make sense to stay so long?" I tossed and turned worrying and was so upset. Eventually I talked to Nick & Laurence and they said it was OK, even good to have us. Anyway, that's what it's like.

TAKE YOUR TIME. Don't write too soon. I won't be ready to write again for a while. Bye for now, Love, Dianne.

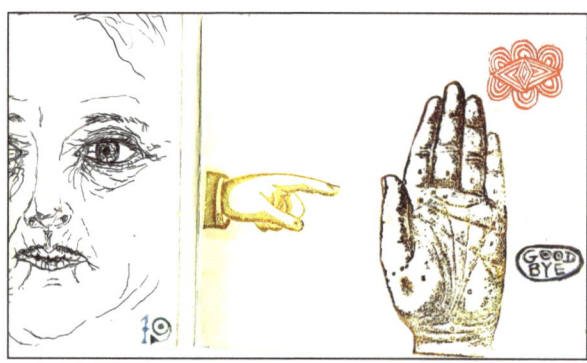

To Bill

I am finally starting your letter. This postcard is a "construction" we saw a few years ago; this large pyramid populated by all kinds of plastic folks—superheroes, Army guys, etc. The title is "Maya." Do you know the term? The artist is one of Norman Rockwell's children.

To Dianne

This is still not a letter, but I've been mulling something. You mentioned being interested in *Places & Stories*, and I wondered if you might like to try your hand at an illustration for one of the stories?

The story is "Dragon's Dilemma," enclosed with this. (It's a sort of Chinese fairy tale.) What I would need would be a full-page drawing (or maybe a full-page rubber stamp!) of Sam the Dragon, perhaps with a tear in his eye.

I am very good at commissioning people to do things for me, with no pay except a credit and a free copy. But I never mind if they beg off. Answer by postcard. A *small* postcard.

To Bill

Pema Chödrön describes our regular lives as standing in a beautiful garden blind-folded.

oh my mind drives me crazy

oh Bill, don't worry. I write when I want to and I just made that last letter a little too long. I'll be more careful next time.

Thanks for sending the old copy of *Oliver Twist*. I was going to start cutting it up but instead have been reading it.

To Bill

Here are some prints of the "Sam" carving. I had trouble getting a good print with a stamp pad, so I used woodblock ink and a brayer. It is possible to color in any white dots with a black pen or pencil. You can cut out the little girl if you want.

To Dianne

Dearest Dianne,

The dragon is perfect! I love it! Certainly white spots in the inking can be touched up with a pen, but that is hardly necessary. As you probably know, Chinese masters always put a flaw in their paintings, so as not to challenge the perfection of God. Another reason not to worry about specks.

Somewhere along the line there will be a letter to you. This isn't it.

To Bill

Hi, Bill. I haven't heard from you for a while and just wanted to check that everything is O.K. on your end. I hope it's

tuesday   october 23, 2007
Dear Bill,
Here are some prints of the
carving.
I had trouble getting a
good print with a stamp
pad so I used wood block
ink & a brayer.
It is possible to color in any
white dots w a black pen
or pencil (as on this one)
you can cut out the
little girl if you want

I hope this fits
the bill — As you
can see it was
fun to do —
I dropped other
projects to do this!
    Bye for now,
    ♡ Dianne

just that you are happy and busy. All is well here, life goes on at its relentless pace and we are pulled along with it.

[Added note] My friend Anne thinks we have some weird psychic connection, since I wrote this postcard this morning a couple of hours before your postcard arrived. Well, there will be no report on India this year. We were to go with Nicholas and his family, but one of Nick's clients is having a first public offering, so he's grounded and so are we. In the meantime, we are going to Dubai right after Christmas when Anne gets back from her Kansas visit with her family. We'll stay in Dubai a week and then spend a week in Istanbul on our way home.

I am writing on a tiny corner of my desk as both cats are here beside me purring as they spread out over my papers and art supplies.

To Dianne

This letter has been a little slow starting itself, but today's the day. Got your postcard, was sorry the India trip had fallen through (for now), but also maybe just a bit relieved that you weren't on the Ganges. India intimidates me—too big, too populous, too poor (and for the same reasons I'd like to go there).

So now a letter. What does Dianne want to hear about? Check off the following:

Christmas prep: Nah, not very interesting.

Firewood: We have a lot of it right now, so we'll have a warm winter. We are firewood snobs—want cherry and walnut if we can get it. Applewood. Ash and oak are always fine. Hackberry is wonderful but rare. So now I can sit up late, with a glass of homemade pear wine, and meditate on fires. "Ashes do not go back to firewood," says the Buddha (or one of his surrogates) and this is true.

Unburdening our lives: The fall projects began with repapering the bedroom. This involved taking down bookshelves from one wall, and then we decided it was time to get rid of some books. Karen priced out 1,040 volumes on an Internet site, and an Indianapolis book dealer took them off our hands for a better price than we expected. Our lives (and house) already feel less stuffed. We're telling people not to give us books for Christmas.

The Zen of trailer rehab: I was supposed to help my church rehab a trailer

today, but messages got mixed (or not delivered), and I ended up sitting in the church basement for an hour waiting for the project honcho to show up. Once I would have stewed about this, but instead I picked out a treatise on Esther from the church library and read it. Wow! What a story! I knew it once, but had forgotten the details and exactly why malefactors are hanged "higher than Haman." Incidentally, Karen says she's always been able to turn off her mind. "Guess I've always been into Zen and didn't know it," she says.

Literary efforts: *Places & Stories*, with your gorgeous dragon, is moving slowly but steadily toward the print-on-demand publisher in Texas. The cover artists (a former student and her boyfriend, both profs at the Savannah School of Design) were in town last week, so we had lunch and went over what they'd come up with. As always, I proposed, the artists disposed—and they came up with a design better than anything I could have envisioned.

Birdhouse gourds: These were the big garden experiment this year. From four or five small hills, they spread out over the adjoining garden and yard, and pretty soon 20 or more gourds were growing away. Some stayed relatively small (wrens). Others got huge (eagles, I think). We picked the last ones just before the first snow. We now have our winter work cut out, boring holes to match the size of birds and shellacking the exteriors. Do you need a birdhouse? Your birds can have one for free, without even a subprime mortgage.

Christmas, 2007

An alligator eating sushi
(ants like sushi, too)
wanted an Arabic portable mixer
so he could fix special food for his
cat.
    The good witch said she would talk
to Santa Claus
    but the royal dog began to bark

so Mr. Incredible came running.
"I'm an American," he said.
So are we, said the monkey.
    But the man in the moon will take
control and
    we will all have a nice holiday—
you and you and you
and us, too. ♥ Dianne, David, Anne

To Dianne

N.A.L.

I suspect you're still out of the country. Or, given our record of synchronicity, you're back and our letters are crossing each other in the mail. Or our non-letters anyway.

Actually, I haven't had time to write much of anything the last few days, since I'm involved in a slightly insane editing project. Someone at the publisher's for whom I edit decided it would be a good idea to have an author write an instant book just before the end of the fiscal year. It would be easy—all he'd have to do would be to change the labels in an earlier book. I would have almost no editing to do, we'd all make money.

You can see where this is going. Nothing, of course, has gone according to plan. It's an "open source" technical book, which is squirrelly to begin with. Some of the needed information, I believe, is available only on a web site run by someone on a mountain in Nepal.

I am standing on a chair (figuratively, at least) and saying "Ommmm" a lot.

There is no pressure for you to write, but you might drop a card and let me know that you got back from Dubai. We have been entertaining another traveler, a houseguest named Flat Stanley, about whom more anon.

To Bill

It feels good to be starting a letter to you, but instead of being at home at my desk I am squeezed into the middle seat on an airplane, trying to juggle my stamps, stamps, stamp pads, colored pencils, and pens on this little folddown tray table. I had determined that I would put off responding to your early December letter until I got back from THE BIG TRIP, but now we have decided—kind of last minute—on another trip.

What happened was that an uncle—the last one of my father's siblings—is having a 90th birthday. I hadn't seen him in a number

...was lush foliage and his house is ½ a block from the ocean on one side and a little more to Lake Worth on the other side.
But even the crummy pastel stucco buildings

THIS IS STAMPING THROUGH A HENNA PATTERN I GOT IN ISTANBUL

have a kind of charm that were lost on my superior New England attitudes as a kid. It's kind of nice to see that one does of years and thought, "He's not going to be around a whole lot longer, so why not go see him?" One special thing about this guy is that his voice is just like my dad's voice—and my dad has been dead 35 years or so.

Anyway, we decide to go, then my brother from New Hampshire decides to go, and other cousins from around. Then, "Hey, we're going to fly to Florida anyhow, so why don't we go exploring? It's been about a million years since we've been there."

So we've got reservations in Miami & Key West and plan to explore the Everglades a bit, too. I graduated from high school here around 1964 or 65 and I hated Florida. I thought the kids were rednecks, anti-intellectual, and that it was very ugly here. This trip is my first time back in 26 years and I am shocked at how nice it is. Even the crummy pastel stucco buildings have a kind of charm that was lost on my superior New England attitudes as a kid. It's kind of nice to see that one does actually see things differently as one ages and changes.

I should make some report on the other trip. Dubai was as it was before, but Istanbul was something else. We were drawn to go over the Galeta Bridge a number of times to see the men fishing and to eat little grilled

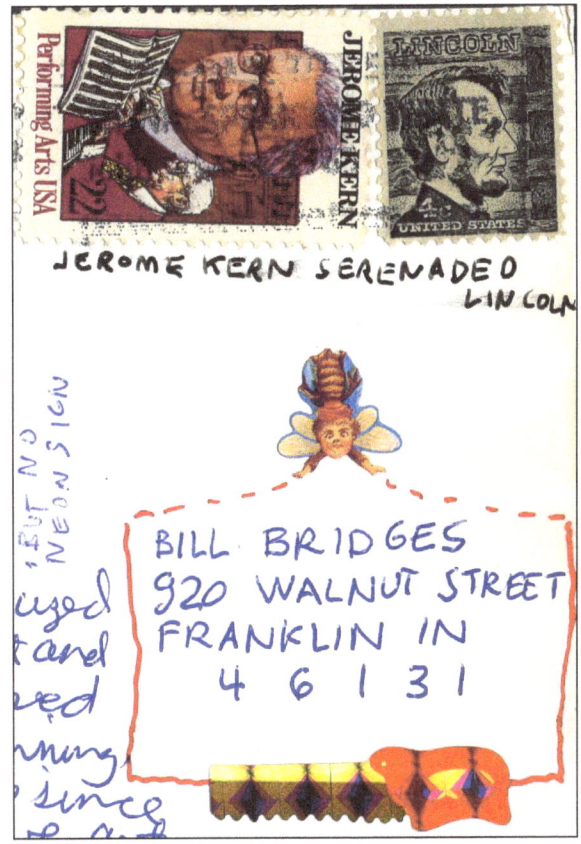

fish sandwiches made on small boats rocking back & forth in the Bosporus. Other high spots were freshly squeezed pomegranate juice made as we waited at a street stall, going to see whirling dervishes whirl, going to the hammam—the Turkish baths where we lay naked on a hot marble plinth while big women scrubbed us, massaged us and shampooed us until we felt sparkling and new.

[Friday] Hello again Dear Bill. We are sitting in an open-air restaurant on the boardwalk along the water in Key West. It's early and quiet and we are in the shade, and although we have ordered breakfast, I hope we can stay put long enough for me to put in some writing on this letter to you. We are planning to visit Ernest Hemingway's house today, which is said to be populated by the offspring of the 50 cats that lived with him. No wonder he shot himself!

The gourds sound terrific, but we've got two cats who pull off any attempt to get a collar with a bell on them, so we don't do bird feeders. Still, each spring they manage to catch a bird or two and that is deeply upsetting. Once in a while they bring one home still slightly alive and I just want to run away and pretend I didn't see it.

One of the good things about being on vacation is that there is no to-do list other than should we eat at that cool seafood place tonight or the tiny French restaurant that the other guidebook wrote about. I hadn't quite caught up from the trip to Dubai and Istanbul, and now I'll be catching up again. But that's next week. Today I am sitting by the water in Key West.

[Later] We are back at our budget hotel and it is not quite 8:30 p.m. This being a tourist is taxing. Key West is a parking nightmare, so we parked our rented Mustang convertible and have been walking everywhere. Between that and having two beers and a Bloody Mary in one day I am pooped. At the Hemingway house there are 47 cats right now & the guide knew all their names and ages. David thinks maybe he was making that up. I don't.

 *To Bill*

I was glad to get your card. It's a good day when we get a piece of "real" mail and not just bills & credit card offers.

We have both had heavy colds since we got home from Florida, but may as well be happy even if we are feeling crappy. See you in the mail.

 *To Dianne*

It looks as if we may be snowed in for a day or two—good time to start a letter.

It's also a good time to step back and collect my thoughts. For a variety of reasons they're somewhat scattered. What scatters them is mainly the different worlds I'm living

81

in at the moment—although there is nothing unusual about this, since everyone experiences it. Think I'm just unusually aware of it right now. If you'll be a captive audience, I'll explain.

One world is that of the Indiana newspaper business, where I'm involved as a mentor for student interns. We had our selection meeting in Indianapolis yesterday, which took the whole day and was difficult—in part because the woman running the day had just flown back at 6 a.m. from San Diego where (as she put it) "I sent my son off to war." She didn't have the selection process very well organized, and who could blame her? The newspaper business everywhere is in great disarray, as it leaves print behind and tries to adapt to the e-world. It's a much different profession than the one I spent my life in, and troubling in many ways.

Another world is that of computer tech-book editing. One book for professional programmers (1,000 pages, 60 chapters) is coming down to deadline and the authors, in Australia, are seriously behind. They're downplaying the problems, but as my brother Steve once said, "When an Aussie says, 'No worries, mate,' it's time to worry."

In addition to this, I'm now facing the prospect of re-editing 25 chapters, just because I asked a question. Should have known better. With Age Comes Wisdom—or should.

SEVERAL BOXCARS OF WISDOM

I have just discovered that this is going to be an illustrated letter—your influence obviously.

Still another world: 10th- and 11th-century Japan. For Christmas, my step-granddaughter Amber gave me *The Tale of Murasaki*. This is a novelized biography of Murasaki Shikibu, author of *The Tale of Genji*, which is the great masterpiece of Japanese literature and the world's first novel. The modern book is a delight, and I told the author so. The author is Liza Dalby, who lives in Berkeley and is the only westerner to have been a geisha. She wrote a nice e-mail back, and spurred by this I've begun reading my copy of *Genji*, which is a bigger challenge than *War and Peace* (or in your case, probably, this letter). Using the time-tested 10-pages-a-day method, I'm closing in on the first 200 pages of this 1,000-page monster.

So what do I bring to this formidable reading task? Well, some basic knowledge of Japan and of Kyoto, where much of the action takes place. Prince Genji lives in the Nijo Palace, which Karen and I have visited. More to the point, living three-quarters of a century (almost) has provided me with some understanding of human nature— valuable, since *Genji* is mainly about relationships between men and women in a highly structured, ritualistic, and utterly male-dominated society. I remarked to Karen that this society sounded pretty good to me, to which she replied, "Dream on."

I also bring some understanding, as an amateur genealogist, of the bizarre webs of

consanguinity in ancient Japan. Only this week, I appealed to my Cousin Ivan for help in more fully identifying one Henningham Clark Nay (pictured here with her husband,

Presley Nay), who I believe may have been a sister of my great-great grandmother. Henningham is also known for having lost her false teeth out the window of a Big Four railway car. The crew stopped the train and retrieved them for her.

Cousin Ivan appealed to a "Cousin Rose" (I don't know who she is, except that she lives in West Virginia), who replied that my great-great grandfather George Bridges's "second wife was Martha Clark, and his first wife was Matilda Forsyth, sister to our John Hume Forsyth and David Forsyth, the first husband of Henningham Clark. Since Bill [that's me] said he was related through Martha Clark, that would make Henningham Clark Forsythe Bridges Nay his step- (with some greats) aunt. I know this is as clear as mud." Indeed. The Japanese have nothing on us.

I could go on trouping through various worlds, but you get the picture. It's a bit frazzling. As someone in the forthcoming *Places & Stories* remarks: "Ideally, there would just be me."

[March 9] We drove to Homer, Indiana, the other day and picked up Jack's refinished piecrust table. I once sent you a picture of little Billy, age 3, with the table in

the background. I thought it would be fun to recreate the scene with the restored table. (Billy, alas, is beyond repair.)

The refinisher did an amazing job—the boss of the business did the project himself and thanked me profusely for letting him work on it. "Your father knew what he was doing," he said. As you can see, it glows—the deepest thanks to you and Anne for bringing it all the way across the country to Franklin.

With the snow moving off, Karen and I got out this afternoon to a concert at the high school by a 23-year-old cellist, Joshua Roman, who is first chair with the Seattle Symphony. His grandparents live in Franklin,

so he suggested a benefit concert for Habitat for Humanity. It was a delight. I'm not a musician at all, but could listen to the cello all day. When I heard Lynn Harrell in Taipei, the audience simply wouldn't let him go. He came back for five encores and before the last one looked quizzically around the proscenium as if to say, "Are you people still here??!!" It was a wild night for cello lovers.

Inserting art certainly makes for longer letters, doesn't it? Although it may not seem like it, I haven't lost track of the fact that this is allegedly in response to your letter of Feb. 1 et seq., which is in front of me. I don't know anyone else who makes accounts of vacation travel as vivid as you do, and it's because you actually see things and aren't self-conscious about describing them (so don't start being self-conscious). I've always had a dream about going to Istanbul, and now I almost feel you've taken me there. Those wonderful little fish from the boats!

[Monday night, 3/10] I suppose I ought to start thinking about winding up this letter. But maybe not just yet. I thought about your trip to Turkey just a few minutes ago when I wandered past the TV and was pulled in by a PBS program on the Bronze

Age and Helen of Troy. What a great countryside for chariots! And there was a highway sign: Troia, 5 km [!]. I was snared early by Helen, in a little *Stories from the Iliad, Told to the Children*, with W. Heath Robinson illustrations, including a delectable though strangely bony Helen gazing out over the Aegean. "Into the sleeping heart of Helen there came remembrance," the caption read. Then a few months ago I read the actual *Iliad* and realized how dripping with gore it was!

Just had another e-mail from Cousin Ivan addressed to "Bill Bridges seen driving red Hornet turning north on Main today."

Life in a small town.

Before leaving family history, I'll tell you about the accompanying picture, which is of Karen's grandparents, Nancy and Silas Enochs, who reared her mother on a little farm near Carlisle, Indiana. Don't they look like a nice old couple? The original photo was in bad shape, but a friend who is a Photoshop wizard worked his magic, and now it's much better. We left the sunflower growing out of Nancy's ear, though.

Think I mentioned having a visit from Flat Stanley. This was a cardboard cutout, the size and shape of a gingerbread cookie, mailed to us by Channing Lee [above], the daughter of friends in California. Our mission: to expose Ms. Stanley to Hoosier culture, show her the sights, photograph her, and send her back home with a report for the first-grade class at Fairmont School, and its teacher, the intrepid Miss Dexter. Mission Accomplished. Photographic proof enclosed.

Speaking of cookies, I sat next to a man in a Chinese restaurant the other day who turned his fortune cookie back in when he paid his bill. Can you imagine being that jaded? I told this to a friend, who said she once received a message that said, "Sorry, wrong cookie." The best one I ever opened said, "Your mind is clear, your heart pure, and your soul sublime." Since then, I've felt there's no place else to go.

P.S. Karen is watching birds in Scotland on a WebCam.

To Bill

THIS IS NOT A LETTER

Hi, Bill,

Thanks for the great mail. I am just recovering from the big Easter/Passover spring party. We had more than 40 guests and all the bunnies I have collected over the years came out for the big day. Now I am in

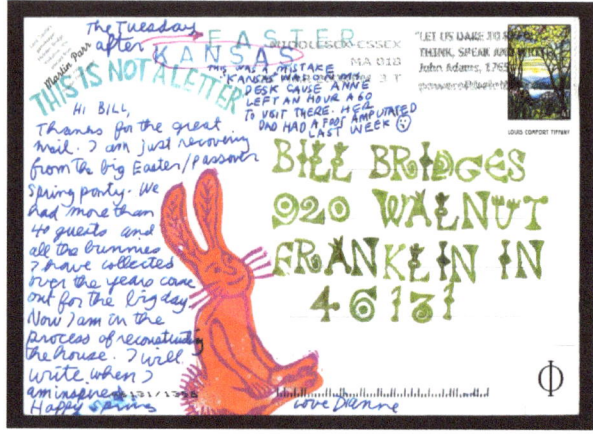

the process of reconstructing the house. I will write when I am inspired. Happy spring.

To Bill

[Bill's note: When I opened the large— 8½ by 11—birthday card below, it turned out to be the collage on the following pages.]

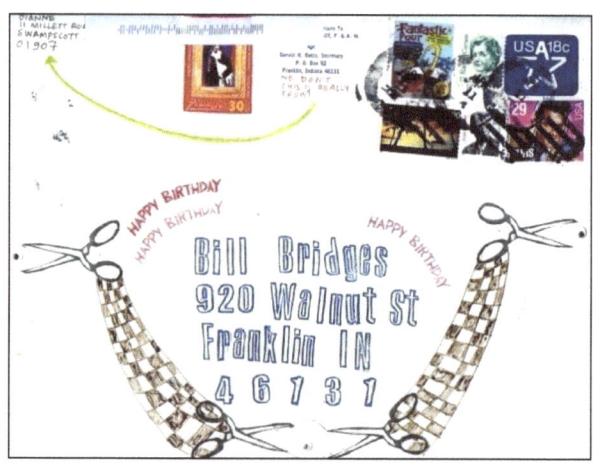

[1] He couldn't hold on to the boat any longer so he set it free

[2] and the two observers, neither of whom had on pants, laughed.

[3] "Well, I think pockets are funny."

[4] But the kid did have pockets, no money though—so he was stuck eating his peanut butter sandwich although he would have much preferred a Chinese luncheon special.

[5] You see, his mother, Marie, had a very low-paying job as a checkout clerk

[6] while his Dad attempted to rise above everyday life by trampolining up up up high and also by diving and swimming down under below

[7] and recording fish songs.

[8] Stop, she called,

[9] come into the darkness with me.

[10] But he couldn't see well.

[11] He had wanted to fly

[12] but now it seems he was turning into a bird—that was what was wrong with his eyesight.

[13] The other birds wanted to cast him out.

[14] But he had discovered the key to their lives

[15] and he put all the information into a small wagon.

[16] His sweetheart sat reading his secrets when a bee came in

[17] and spoke to him about the twins, who looked less and less alike until

[18] they all seemed to forget about him.

[19] I will walk along the beach. The sound of the waves is soothing. I will think about the birds and I will remember my purpose here on earth.

[20] But he did forget

[21] and so did he

[22] and he forgot

[23] "I forgot, too."

[24] I could listen to your music. It's thoughtful of you to come and play for me [25] but I hate that tune.

[26] So more exploring for me beyond the beyond

[27] where Mamie waits for me

* * *

[April 10] Dear Bill, Well I am finally here. I have been ready to write for a while but waiting for a quiet time when no one is at home to interrupt my flow of thought. And now I am afraid there will be no flow of thought.

Years ago I saw (and kept for a long time) a cartoon of a person at a crossroads. One sign pointed to YOUR DREAMS COME TRUE, the other pointed to A COOLER PERSON'S DREAMS COME TRUE. That stuck with me.

So first let me say something about this THING [the big birthday card] I am sending you. Recently I got into gluing pictures from my collage books—playing around with cutting out images and stamping and maybe cutting out a few phrases and then writing some kind of story to go along with the images. This has been very casual and fun. Then I thought, maybe I could do one on a big page and then I can hang it up. So I put one together and it is sitting here not complete and suddenly it feels like a BIG DEAL and all the parts of me that say YOU ARE NO ARTIST are fighting to get to me first to yell their messages about what a stupid presumptious amateur I am and how dare I even consider making REAL ART. Somehow they accept my making daily pages and making mail but that's it.

This is my chief critic. For a while she has left me alone but she is on my case bigtime right now. And I am extremely wound up wanting to work at my desk. But of course there are all kinds of other commitments and promises. So, that's where I am at.

I loved your stories about Genji. I tried to read it some years ago and gave up, but maybe I should try your ten pages a day. I love that you have the photos in your letter of the various folks. Karen's grandparents in particular are lovely. Nancy Enochs surely has some downhome cooking almost ready to serve.

Today is the warmest day of the year. It is so mild that I am sitting at Anne's desk with the door open. Ah spring. And how funny that one can watch birds on WebCam. What a wonderful world this is. Wonderful and terrible.

Yesterday I cut out a drawing of a kid blindfolded chasing another kid. Something about blindfolded people appeals to me. So I started a big drawing, to be painting, and now I think I'll do a carving and then I will stamp it on here.

So there I am—don't exactly know where I'm going but I'm going fast and trying to make art about it.

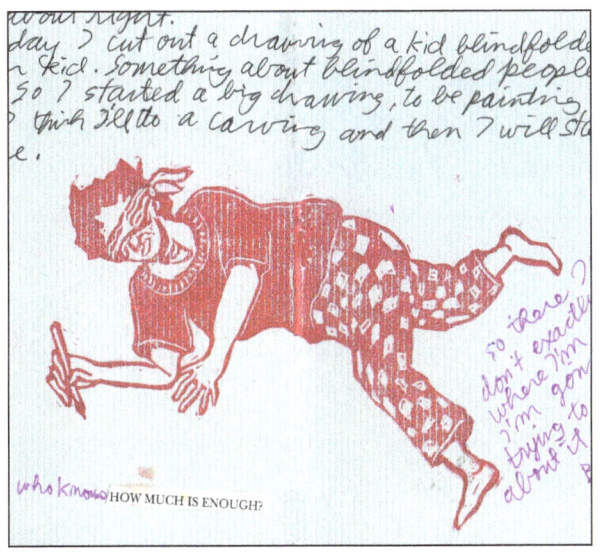

 **To Bill**

oh Bill,

Thank you for the book [*Places & Stories*]. What a lovely thing to get in the mail. This is not a letter, but just to let you know we got it. It looks wonderful and I hope to get down to some actual reading next week.

 **To Dianne**

This is SORT OF A LETTER, though a shorter one than usual.

With *Places & Stories* out of the way, I'm starting to think again of the idea we tossed around briefly, many months ago, of putting together letter excerpts and your art in a book. This was always very tentative, and as time went on the letters have been so much fun that I didn't want to think of them as a project.

But now I am thinking again of some sort of publication—if you're willing to explore this idea some more. Are you intrigued, interested, appalled? If the last, a firm "no" will be sufficient. Otherwise all suggestions are welcome. At bottom, I simply love your art and your letters—and when I love something, I want to make art myself.

To Bill

I got your nice letter proposing to do something with our mail and art. COOL. I am delighted with the idea and will do whatever you ask (well, within certain parameters) to make it happen. One thing that happens for me is that I generally don't remember too much of what I have made and sent out. One time I was at my friend's house in Los Angeles and I picked up this little booklet and thought it was very

interesting and on further examination saw that it was something I had made for her.

The board on which this is written was something I salvaged from someone's garbage when I was taking a walk in Salem. It was part of a game. I like the way it folds, but it is resistant to art materials.

Anne has been in Kansas for almost 3 weeks tending to her parents—her dad had a stroke and had a foot amputated. She comes home tonight and we plan to take a number of short trips before summer school starts & my Dubai family arrives. Things are blooming here. Happy Spring.

[Note] I don't know exactly what I'm doing. The picture is my new tattoo on my left arm.

To Dianne

Thanks so much for the "game board" letter and the go-ahead.

I've been meaning to write for a couple of days, but things have been a little confused here, since we're in the middle of one of the worst floods in 100 years. In the middle, but not in the flood. We've had no problems beyond a drowned garden and the loss of land-line phone service.

But it's been a strange week anyway. This all began Friday night with 10 inches of rain in 12 hours, eclipsing the state record set in 1905. Our street was running bank to bank for a while, and "Lake Northwood" quickly formed on the athletic field of Northwood School, just behind us. Soon we had ducks and children splashing. We're on

high ground, so the street soon cleared, but the lake came up into our backyard for the first time ever.

Still it was just high water—but things downtown turned out to be much worse. The creeks in that part of the city went crazy, cresting at 14 feet or more, the highest in history. Government offices and the police station were wiped out (along with most of the police cars and computers). People lost their homes. Friends had eight feet of water in their basement and a foundation wall collapsed. This was all going on a mile from us, and we would have been barely aware of it, except for the massive TV and newspaper coverage.

What we have been painfully aware of is the plight of friends whose house is in the country east of town. They left last week on an Alaskan cruise to celebrate their 50th wedding anniversary. We're in charge of watering plants, but when we went out Sunday they had a foot of water in their finished basement, even though four sump pumps were running. What to do. Should we call them home from Alaska? A plumber has advised doing nothing until the water recedes. Stay out of the basement, he warned—danger of electrocution. But we've been doing a lot of agonizing (which I've now passed on to you!).

One project came to an end last week— the 10-pages-a-day slogging through *The Tale of Genji*. Fascinating in a way and sort of a Zen exercise, but I don't necessarily recommend it. I've been coming back from ancient Japan with the help of *The Other Wind*, Ursula LeGuin's new addition to the Earthsea books. Her take, via fantasy, on life and death.

All the best to David and to Anne in her bad patch with her Dad. Sounds as if you have a busy time coming up, with travel and visitors, so I won't expect any major art objects soon.

To Dianne

Dearest Dianne,

And also David and Anne, whom I enjoy thinking of as looking over your shoulder while you read. David is probably the oldest friend with whom I am still in any sort of touch. I still have very clear memories of playing at his house on Buntin Street (where I once knocked myself out by falling on the front sidewalk and had to be revived in the doctor's house across the street).

This is an odd way to start a letter, but I think I'm in the spot you were several months back, of not especially wanting to hear my own voice. I have been looking through our letters of the last two years, and thinking about how "the project" might

unfold. Your letters (and the art) are as much a delight the second time as the first, and there are some themes that might tie it together—the nature of creativity (both in art and writing), what travel contributes to this, the importance (or not) of audience, Zen thought as a sort of matrix. Very vague so far, but I'm seeing some threads.

I approach making books in something the same spirit as reading *The Tale of Genji*—one takes the first step, then the next. Eventually it gets done, as long as one doesn't think about it too much.

Meanwhile, other things go on. Our friends got back from Alaska and have taken all the steps to get their basement dried out and the waterlogged trash disposed of. The rest of the town seems to be recovering—except that I'm having mixed feelings about the coverage of the emergency in the local paper. We have had nothing (that's right, literally nothing) on the front page, or most of the inside pages, for two weeks except disaster and recovery news. We've had front-page spreads on everything from the first "flood baby" to the plight of homeless dogs and cats. There is now a place non-flooded residents can go to get counseling for survivor guilt. As a cynical journalist who praised the news coverage at first, I'm beginning to get a whiff of "let's win a prize." But I am probably just an Old Curmudgeon.

We are sort of lolling through the summer. The garden is thriving under benign neglect. About our most exciting activity is bird-watching. A robin began nesting early in the spring, on a tiny bit of space near the front-porch ceiling, just above where the swing usually goes. I nailed up a wooden strip so Mama would have a little more support, and she raised two broods before finally abandoning the nest a few days ago. We saw it all from our bedroom window!

On the lit'ry front, I just sent off a collection of poems to a chapbook competition at Georgetown, Ky. My writing friend Susanna has also entered. Georgetown is only a few miles from Winchester, Ky., where son Mike and his wife Amanda live. When I told Mike about the contest, he said, "Hey, I'll get da boys and we'll go over and destroy all the entries except yours and Susanna's." Then he added, "Don't worry, we'll make it look like an accident."

What a concept! Poets with their own "muscle"!

End of page, end of almost-letter.

 *To Bill*

As you can see by my being a month behind, I have been having some trouble with TIME. ZIP it's here and ZIP it's gone.

Your last letter ended without a signature. I wondered if you forgot to print the last page. At any rate I am glad for the letter.

Anne and I have had a whole bunch of little trips. The longest a week in San

IN THE AIR AND INTO THE WATER

Thomas Henry Huxley

I am sure it is all connected somehow

Copy't Dupont
CALVE AS CARMEN

PARKING METER HEAD FROM STORE IN BELLINGHAM WASHINGTON

WOODEN BEAR TOOTHPICK HOLDER

If we only knew the real value of the day.

keep in touch

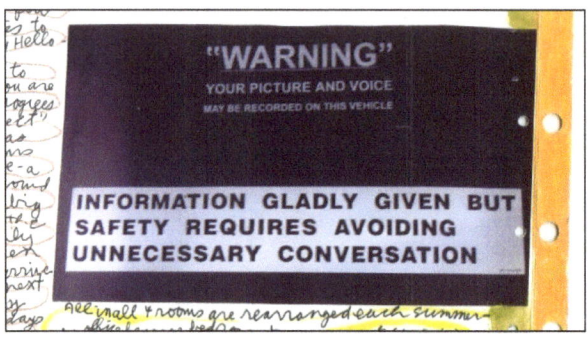

Francisco where I got the accompanying photo about unnecessary conversation on a trolley car, while traveling on one. I could make numerous copies of that and put them around the house, but really isn't unnecessary conversation one of life's

greatest pleasures? Actually I like all kinds of unnecessities.

I have been dragging this letter around for more than a week, hoping for a few quiet minutes to at least say Hello. I am excited to hear that you are making progress on "The Project." Company has been—seems always to be—a constant around here. The big visit from the Dubai family begins when the ladies arrive from Paris next Monday & my son arrives 3 days later. They will be here for a 3-week marathon of eating, going to museums, the beach, etc. We have been doing our annual house rearranging so that everyone has the right bedroom. Parents must be on a different floor than children so said parents can sleep. Grandma sleeps nearby to hear the kids. All in all, 4 rooms are re-arranged each summer. An office becomes a bedroom, etc.

Meanwhile I have been reading novels & such at the beach. Ann Patchett & Murakami are favorite authors this summer. Oh no, out of room already. Be well, enjoy.

To Dianne

It's not the season for nice big sprawling letters here either—but I do want to acknowledge the beautiful "potato

CUT

CUT

CUT

faces" letter and bring you up to date a little with things here. NAR—No answer required.

I've had a Revelation. I was thinking that photographing your mail-art would be a pretty demanding process, and limiting in how much I could do. Then the revelation—I can put your letters directly on my new flatbed scanner and get instant computer files, in high-quality color.

There have been other revelations as I got into this. Your letters and art have proved to be highly dynamic—I found myself "excerpting" in ways that created something new. It's interesting that bits of writing take on a different life when "framed" next to the art. Or it seems to me they do. What do you think about this?

You've disparaged your handwriting at times, but if you can distance yourself a bit, I think you may see it as I do—a very human "hand" that seems at home with the neighboring art. And quite legible. (If you aspired to the Spencerian, you should have spent more time at Miss Brody's School for Young Ladies.)

I love typing on the Rem because I get to correct my errors visibly and they become part of the letter. Well, I don't know for sure where all this is going—and if I did, it wouldn't be any fun. The art/letter catalog is progressing, but it's probably gotten about as far as it will before we leave for Scotland on 8/16.

I have been sharing your feelings about time and its rapid passage. I don't know what to do about it either—on one level I know I will die with things undone, so it doesn't matter. But I'm not very good at convincing myself of that. Started a to-do list today, but wrote at the top, "Let Buddha do it." Maybe that could be a stamp someday (but not soon).

Unnecessary conversations are often the best kind. Mike O'Connor, my poet friend out in Port Townsend, Washington, is

thinking of titling his memoir *Talks Unnecessarily*, from the comment on his primary school report cards. That would be a wonderful title, but he's afraid it might be too cryptic.

DANGER! This could be becoming a letter. Time to quit. You'll get at least a card from Scotland.

PS I think I just forgot to sign the last one. Of course I could say that the really good stuff was on the missing page.

To Bill

Hello Bill. Thanks for the various mails you've sent. I am currently in the catching up mode so a longer letter will have to wait a bit longer. But I wanted to be sure to let you know that every piece of mail from you is treasured. We had a hectic and satisfying visit with the Dubai family. Anne and I then spent a week in NYC. A real letter soon.

To Bill

[*Homemade card with a pocket, enclosing strip with people and animals yakking it up. Legend: Talk is cheap because the supply exceeds the demand.*]

Cleaning house. This is an old card. I used to send these out, cards by subscription. It never really worked as a

Did you hear about the duck who went into a drugstore and said:

"Give me some chapstick and put it on my bill."

BILL BRIDGES
920 WALNUT
FRANKLIN IN
46131

business, but it was fun.

Thanks for the card from Scotland. Welcome home. I started a letter to you today so you can expect it one of these days.

To Bill

THIS IS NOT A LETTER. But I am writing one to you today. Did you hear about the duck who went into a drugstore and said: "Give me some chapstick and put it on my bill"?

To Dianne

As you can see, we made it back safely from Scotland. The trip went almost exactly as planned, although we got a lot of rain.

But this was Scotland, after all, and we'd been exceptionally lucky weatherwise on earlier trips. I won't give you the lengthy "what I did on my summer vacation" report. Enough to say that we got to all the places we planned, and reunited with various friends. Edwin Wakeling, the husband of a woman whom I was on St. Kilda with in 2000, is a retired reindeer herder. He and his wife, Ann, took granddaughter Rebecca and me to a reindeer pasture in the Cairngorm Mountains. Rebecca got to feed reindeer and was in heaven. Edwin reminisced about his days with the herd just after it was

imported from Lapland in the late 1950s. Says he spent most of his time wandering in vast upland pastures, wondering where the reindeer were. "It got easier once I started thinking like one," he said.

Ann also did a few natural history lessons as we went along, showing Rebecca berries from a rowan tree and explaining that the Celts used to apologize to the tree for taking them.

We also got together for lunch near Inverness with Bob Will, an archaeologist from Kilda, and his wife Susan, who is the chief archaeologist for the Western Isles.

The big hit of the trip was Rebecca. We didn't know what traveling with a 12-year-old girl would be like, not having any experience in that area. But she was wonderful—loved everything and everybody, and energized us old folks.

When we got back to Edinburgh, I went to the Gallery of Modern Art, hoping to see work by a fine Scottish artist, Joan Eardling. Alas, there had just been a big exhibition of it, and all her stuff was temporarily off the walls. But I did see some pretty strange art by a Tracey Emin, whose work included a display of her messy room and unmade bed. "Just think," Colin said when I described

it. "All those years at home we were making art and didn't know it."

The other piece of art we saw—magnificent!—was the Falkirk Millennium Wheel, a giant boat lift built several years ago to replace nine locks on the cross-Scotland canal. A Ferris wheel for boats. We rode it up 35 meters to the upper canal, and it was like traveling inside a Henry Moore sculpture, with huge cast concrete balance wheels and lots of interesting gears.

On the way home we stopped off in New York for a couple days to visit Colin. Took the 3-hour Circle Line cruise around Manhattan, had lunch in Bryant Park, and visited the International Center of Photography. Good time had by all. Then we skedaddled for home, an hour or so ahead of Tropical Storm Hanna.

On other fronts: I've resumed the door-to-door campaigning for Obama that began in the primary. Hadn't really planned to do this, but there seems to be a real push on to do well in Indiana, so I've enlisted again. I have to respect and admire McCain for his wartime heroism, but he does seem to like shooting from the hip. (Tina Fey was a riot as Sarah Palin on SNL—totally unfair and hilarious. Hope you saw it.)

I'm delving into a monster of a book called the *Ambonese Curiosity Cabinet*, a volume of Far Eastern natural history written 300 years ago by Georgius Eberhardus Rumphius, and only recently translated into English. He died in 1702 before any of his work reached print—one manuscript perished in a fire, another went down when a ship sank, and then the Dutch

government forbade publication for a few years—it feared some of his descriptions of flora and fauna might aid the enemy!

I think I just ran out of grist for this letter. Karen and I are about to go out to the neighborhood Chinese restaurant for some hot-and-spicy soup on a gray, post-Hurricane Ike day.

To Bill

Finally,

HELLO BILL

THIS IS A LETTER

First off I will say that it's too far to write across all this space (the 2 pages that is) so I will just do this bit. I haven't written to you for so long that I have a little stage fright. What am I going to write about and will it have MEANING? Well, the MEANING

be damned. Yesterday on my daily page I declared myself not going to focus on whether my work has consistency, meaning, or value—I have not agreed with myself how long I will let myself go without those concerns but I never seem to get them figured out and why not take a little vacation from them?

I love apologizing to the tree in Scotland. Years ago we did a walk with someone who said they knew about Devas, the spirits of the trees and flowers. They suggested that we ask permission before picking flowers. Not necessarily out loud, but internally and we would feel a response. I think I do sometimes feel that a weed is pleased and flattered to be taken home and put into a vase to be admired. And on occasion I have had the sense that a plant wanted to be left as it was.

The news lately with McCain and his vice president lady has been kind of scary. Our liberal newspapers are good at weeding out her bad points but it seems like a lot of people have fallen in love with her.

OK enough. Something else. I have a tattoo of this blindfolded artist on my arm and tomorrow I am getting a new tattoo (with the artist tracing a colorful spiral). I'm thinking it will be something to the effect of the accompanying sketch with different colors and the spiral on my upper arm. So far my tattoos are all black. This addition will complete my arm (sort of,

So here are most of the typewriters. I have had them all out on a table for a few weeks but they overwhelm the room they are in so I am currently packing them back in carrying cases to be stacked back up in a 3rd floor bedroom.

MY GRANDSON, JACOB, WITH PART OF THE RULER AND YARDSTICK COLLECTION WHICH HE USES IN COMBINATION WITH BLOCKS. IT IS FUN TO WRITE ONE LETTER IN EACH BOX EXCEPT IT IS VERY SLOW. SO FAR I THINK THIS IS A LAME LETTER. BUT I CAN'T START

I guess you can always add more). Maybe then I'll stop.

[Next few lines written on graph paper squares.] Here is a photograph of my grandson, Jacob, with part of the ruler and yardstick collection which he uses in combination with blocks. It is fun to write one letter in each box except it is very slow. So far I think this is a lame letter. But I can't start over because I invested too much effort in creating the form. Sometimes there is something very labor intensive and elaborate in an art gallery and it doesn't add up to much.

That's my fear. She likes to make stuff but it doesn't mean anything.

So much for giving it up.

Can I make things just for the fun of it?

Here is another piece from our typewriter collection. We recently disassembled an electric typewriter that we found in someone's garbage. It took a long time and a number of tools. This essential piece, the type-bar assemblage, with all the keys, has such a lovely feel in your hand. If you come and visit sometime I will give it to you to hold in your hand.

The typewriter on this page was found at a JUNQUE store—not quite an antique store but it had pretensions.

So here are most of the typewriters. I have had them all out on a table for a few weeks, but they overwhelm the room they are in so I am currently packing them back in

carrying cases to be stacked back up in a 3rd floor bedroom.

I started this on Wednesday sitting in the waiting room at the Tattoo parlour and now it is the next day and the tattoo is engraved into my arm for the rest of my life.

[Thursday] This letter is a little screwy in terms of continuity. I began at the beginning but then I jumped around so that part of what I wrote yesterday is after what I am writing today. It may not matter all that much . . . .

It is a lovely sunny day today and I am home alone with only Tootsie, the dog, and Tigger, the cat. Somehow knowing I am home alone and there is no one in another room gives me a lovely sense of well being. It is almost 9:30 however and so far I have been tidying up and starting some laundry and making lists of things to do.

Along with other things on the list I should add to get back to some kind of meditation. Last weekend we had some overnight guests, OLD friends all older than me. I pulled out this saying to see if anyone had an idea:

**Since death alone is certain
and the time of death is uncertain
what should I do?**

What should I do? But no one chose to comment so I guess I'll just go on as I have up until now until the end.

Wednesday early a.m. I've been thinking again about Chuck Close, the artist who said art for art's sake is masturbatory. (I don't know if that's a word or if I spelled it right.) He said he wouldn't make art on a desert island. His paintings sell for millions of dollars, but I doubt he is painting just for the money. Anyway, that's the stuff that's rolling around in my head and now it's 6 a.m. & time to go for a walk.

This is a sketch of the beach we walk to every morning. I remember very clearly that we all walked over to that beach when you

were here with Colin for Marie's Gone to Glory party. It was a cold sunny day and every once in a while I come across the photo of you and David over there on the wall looking out at the ocean.

SACRED ORDINARY SACRED ORDINARY

These words were my first tattoo, around my wrist. At the time I felt certain that our lives were both ORDINARY and SACRED. Some days lately I think perhaps I was fooling myself and it is all just ORDINARY, but it is all so mysterious and so much is so beautiful.

GOOD BYE

FOR NOW

May you have a happy heart
Love, Dianne

*I hope it doesn't horrify you that I cut up dictionaries.

 SEPTEMBER 21

To Dianne

[Written on gift wrap]

Once in a while it seems I have to poach on your turf a little—and I had this nice paper that originally wrapped Karen's birthday nightgown from Von Maur's. (Von Maur is my favorite department store because it stocks Godiva chocolates and has a piano player. It reminds me of the old L.S. Ayres in Indianapolis, which David may remember.)

So . . . this is not the kind of letter that needs an answer, but it is a letter sort of, because I wanted to respond to your feelings about art and audience. I do think some artists would keep on creating (properly so) on a desert island. I would like to think the work itself matters, even if no one sees it.

Some confirmation of this came in an unusual way today. A former student showed up with two books for me, both bearing on the work of a somewhat reclusive poet, William Bronk. One is of letters between Bronk and an artist, Herman Maril. In one letter, Bronk writes: "The problem with public recognition is that it is the artist who becomes important, not the art. The public will never know anything about the art or care about it, though many private persons may or a few may. . . . It is hard for the work to continue when the order of importance is reversed and the artist himself begins to take a solemn view of himself. The public be damned and the artist be damned also. If anything at all matters it is the work only that matters."

In any event, you are not a desert-island artist, and have people who are interested in your work, for the sake of the work. I am savoring the latest "book letter" and will respond more fully. Meanwhile, here are messages for others on Millett Road.

To Anne (who is the chief typewriter collector, I believe): The typewriters are wonderful! Ah, to own an Oliver! But I don't really want to own one. I prefer savoring the prospect.

To David (in his role of theologian): Going door to door on the campaign trail today with a professor of religion who is also named David, we encountered a woman who said she would not vote for anyone who wasn't committed to removing the Palestinians from the Holy Land. David explained later that she was a "dispensationalist pre-millennarian," an extreme fundamentalist Christian who believes Christ won't return until all the Palestinians are kicked out. There are strange things in the Hoosier suburbs. And now I'm out of space.

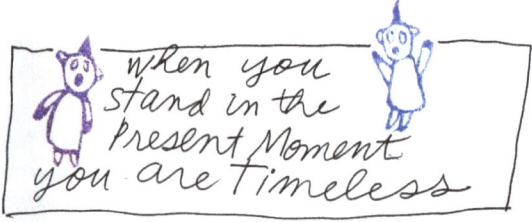

To Bill

Thank you for your letter of 9/15. It seems like our letters crossed as they so often do. I had no idea you were taking Rebecca to Scotland. I'm sure she will remember the trip for her whole life. Yes, we know Tracey Emin's work. She had a tent with embroidery of "All the people I've slept with." We also went to the Int'l Photo Ctr. They always have interesting stuff. Hey, I'm in the middle of stuff & just remembered this was just to say: LATER.

To Dianne

This is still not a reply to your big "book" letter of 9/8. You are still off the hook. What it is is my catalog of our correspondence from April 6, 2006, through June 26, 2008, plus a CD with art from that period.

You've mentioned not keeping track of what you've sent, or even remembering it in detail. So it will probably be a shock to see it cataloged, with sometimes-fanciful names assigned to the items ("Napkin Letter," "Pearl-Button Letter," "Turtle Note," etc.), and capsules of the contents. The apparatus may seem a bit much—I can only plead that it's necessary in order to pull a book together. Or at least it's necessary for me, since I can't hold this much stuff in my feeble head.

This may be about as far as I get before Christmas. When there's eventually some sort of draft (spring, maybe?), I'm thinking seriously of coming out for a couple of days so we can talk over content, layout, design, etc., if that would be okay with you.

At the moment some other things are on the plate here—Norwegian novels, freelance editing, campaigning for Obama, getting the yard and garden buttoned up for winter. (Just stacked a couple of cords of firewood—if the world goes to hell in a new Depression, we'll at least be warm.) More

about all these items in the eventual Real Letter.

P.S. You knew all about Tracey Emin. Why am I not surprised?

 *To Bill*

I am quite bowled over by the CD you sent, by all the energy you have put into this project and by seeing my art work that way. It has stirred up all kinds of feelings , and some understanding of how much I value our correspondence. I will write about all that when I get to a letter. Meanwhile

THANKS

MY DEAR BILL,

I constructed and decorated this letter some time ago and I have been waiting to write you...

OCTOBER 26

To Bill

My Dear Bill,

I constructed and decorated this letter some time ago and I have been waiting to write you until I cleared the decks of some other things. I only looked briefly at the CD when you first sent it, and it was emotional for me. Again this morning I sat down and began to look at the images, but I stopped after a while because somehow they made me feel like crying. I so appreciate your work to make this book thing. I have had a vivid correspondence with various people over the years and of course I never again

see what I send away and thankfully I forget what I have made—often when someone thanks me for a piece of mail I have no idea what they are referring to, only the memory that I recently sent them something. Now it may be that my forgetting what I sent is just old age memory loss but I like to think I am so zen and detached that I just let things go.

This touches on an issue that I am grappling with right now; maybe if I write about it I will get clearer. In May I am planning to have a little art show in a gallery at the library in Marblehead, the next town over from us. Part of what I want to do is expose the dolls to people out in the world. They mostly live in our house and I think

This doll reminds me of the illustrations of an mostly children's book author named Maira Kalman. I've been considering just boxing her up and sending her to that lady—

12

I looked up Susie F... and couldn't get into i... looked at it as ... letter and ... liked it ... while ... you ... on A... used ... Ric... kn... Bill... Who... Tra...

I'd I've

bottles, suitcases and ordinary around-the-house things that are painted here at 11 Millett. Maybe they will be part of the show and maybe not.

The other thing is that we have lots of collections. I have a lint jar collection that started because there is no room for a trash container in the laundry room and rather than go back and forth I started putting lint in jars. They looked good. Voila, a collection.

How did I get here? Oh yeah the other collections. Another collection is houses, mostly small wooden houses that for some reason there are a lot of to be found at yard sales and thrift stores. So I paint them and glue stamps or buttons or something on them. And then there are doll houses and I have gotten a couple lately and have ideas for refurbishing them.

So I talked to the library director about having some sort of an interactive installation with a dollhouse or dollhouses and a few dolls that could be handled, and this morning I started to play with the idea of dollhouse dolls and I found some spools and I drilled holes and can attach beads & use pipecleaners, and the flood/rush of ideas just gushed in and I don't know what to do first.

they need to get out a bit. If anyone wanted to buy one I would be happy to have some money as well, but that is pretty low on reasons for showing. Besides the dolls I am doing some work on wooden panels that I may show, but they are enough like PAINTINGS—real ART—that the parts of me that say "Who the hell do you think you are?" get all stirred up and keep me from working on them. The other thing is the idea of life in art or art in life—all the mouthwash

jars. They looked good. ✓
How did I get here?

so I talked to the librar
Director about having sot

Meanwhile there is laundry to do. Tootsie poops in a certain spot in the living room and that needs to be scrubbed and what will we have for lunch when Anne runs in between schools. And my son Alex's mother-in-law just called from New Jersey to tell me all about their upcoming trip to China. They leave tomorrow for a 19-day tour.

And now I remember why I started to talk about that exhibit at the library.

I want to do this section of the show with stuff that people can play with and arrange, and the people around me are all worried that things will be hurt stolen broken. And I don't know if I should consider that or what. These things are just things and I break lose give away stuff all the time. Anyway I'm kind of lost here. I just looked at this piece of the letter and was trying to figure out how it's going to go together and then I remembered that it has an outer part that this fits in.

OK, back to the BILL-DIANNE correspondence project. Again, WOW, you are putting so much love and care into this I am very appreciative. I think I am repetitive and say the same things over and over and I wonder what it will be like to read our words. Occasionally I think I should do things more carefully and thoughtfully, but no.

Looking at the photos of the letters chokes me up somehow. I like them. I like that I get to see them again, they are like children who have gone off to live their lives and then you see them again and you overflow with love for them and you appreciate them in some new way because you have not seen them and you forgot how much you like them.

It's a little weird to talk about the letters as children but is it that way for you

when you finish a book and send it out into the world? I guess it is different somewhat with a book because even though you send it away you still have it. Well, I love what you

are doing with our letters and I thank you and wish all blessings for you.

Of course it would be lovely for you to come in the spring. The only thing on the calendar now is the library show. I told the library director about our project and she said, "Oh, maybe he could give a little talk at the library. An author!" I guess we'll see how it all unfolds.

Bye for now Lovey, Dianne

[On back] Oh shit, I just noticed that there are two pieces of mail from you that I haven't responded to yet. Next time.

OCTOBER 27 *To Dianne*

This is actually the start of a letter. I have a few minutes before heading off to the dentist for an application of "bond" to restore some surface to a couple of worn teeth. It makes me think of the front-porch repairs Mike and Amanda made to their house in Winchester, Ky. The porch looked pretty good, but they discovered that the previous owner had patched it together with chickenwire and something called "Bond-O." That's how I intend to get through my

golden years, with chickenwire and Bond-O. So what else is on my alleged mind this morning? Museums actually.

The Indianapolis Museum of Art opened a display of Ming artifacts yesterday, and it will run through Jan. 11. "Power and Glory: Court Arts of China's Ming Dynasty," it's called. The Ming is a little too much power and glory for my taste—am more of a T'ang man myself—but I think Karen and I will have to go see it. I haven't been to the IMA for several years. The last time was with Colin to see an exhibition of Moghul art—the Ming will have to go some to top that.

At the other end of the museum spectrum are the little out-of-the-way places that you'd miss if you weren't paying attention. We went to one in Linlithgow, Scotland, commemorating the Edinburgh-Glasgow canal. (Have to interject here that a cab driver told us, "A Glasgow funeral is more fun than an Edinburgh wedding.") The museum was one room, all of 12 feet square, beside the canal, but with some endearing old photos of canal boats and workmen of bygone days. We had to hike to the top of a hill to find it, and I heard plenty about that: "You dragged us all the way up here, for this?" "Yep, and isn't it great?" We also got to watch a wedding party taking off by canal boat, and that in itself was worth the museum entrance cost (about 50 cents, US). Did you know that early canals were built on the tops of hills? I didn't, but it makes sense. They followed ridge lines like early roads, and you never had to worry about your canal flooding.

And now it's time to go bond with my dentist. This little confetti poem, made with potato stamps, will hold the space.

A thin crowd of stars goes out the opening door of a crescent moon.

* * *

PRINCESS PARKING LOT. ALL OTHERS WILL BE TOAD

That's one of the signs I've seen as I trudged around neighborhoods, knocking on doors for Obama. Which is a back-handed way of reporting on the wind-up of the political season here. There will be a few more stops to make next weekend, and I'll be helping coordinate get-out-the-vote volunteers on election day. But I'm starting to have a sense of finality about it. Win or lose, it will soon be over—and I'm not as sure as the polls that Obama holds an edge.

For me it's a road that began on the night of March 18, when I listened to Obama's Philadelphia speech about race, "A More Perfect Union," on my computer. It was the most courageous political speech I had heard in my lifetime, and I ran downstairs, got my wallet, and sent off $100 to the campaign. That got me on the train, and what a ride it's been—in ways I couldn't have imagined. For a journalist, seeing a little of the phenomenal Obama organization from the inside has been worth the price of admission (which is now holding at $400—I believe he has enough money).

Final garden report: The harvest is in. Turnip crop was a huge success, the onions middling. The last lone tomato was picked last week, and the first freeze is scheduled tonight. Most flowers are gone, but marigolds are hanging on and the cosmos are making their last defiant shout against winter. I like annuals more than perennials—they give out everything in one season and then move on.

TUESDAY NIGHT 10/28

I went back tonight and reread your "book" letter of September 8. I love the care with which you put these together. The formats are always a delight, and then the letters themselves are a sort of lagniappe with their own appeal and interest to a writer. And in my case a writer who worries some of the same questions of meaning and the use of time and energy. And finds no satisfying answers either. I believe a Hebrew sage once spoke of our lives as sea voyages in which we are given no destination, but are traveling nonetheless "under mysterious orders not to come in."

The writers I care most about are those who seem to live with that ambivalence, and who have explored it in ways I'm not capable of. I'm a dabbler in these waters. My lifelong problem with religion has been its insistence that there are definite answers we can win through to by faith. I agonized over this for years, like everyone else. Then

a few months ago, it came to me in some way (not a voice, but a distinct conviction) that "you are released from thinking about theology ever again." And I haven't. And am much happier.

While that's freed up my mind considerably, it doesn't answer your concerns about meaning and "what should I do"? All I know to do is to continue living this "weird unfathomable ordinary everyday life," as your stamp says. Perhaps that's exactly what we're supposed to be doing. This also seems to be at the heart of Zen, with its advice to be present and attentive in the moment. A much tougher assignment than it looks.

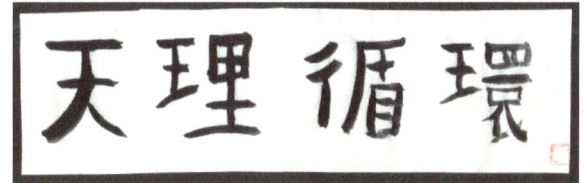

And one can always follow the wisdom of my favorite Chinese "Four Character" saying (above): "The guilty are always punished and the kind-hearted always rewarded, under the law of Heaven." The Chinese say a lot in a small space.

On upsetting news: Take it from a journalist and don't worry about it. For a long time, I had a clipping of a newspaper column headed, "I never read a newspaper and you shouldn't either." Yes, I read newspapers and listen to TV news, but always with the knowledge that this is a business not to be taken too seriously. It thrives on novelty, and I know all its tricks (and have practiced most of them at one time or another). I get most of my news these days from the *New York Review of Books*. It will get around to the election in a month or two and tell me what really happened, or give me clues to figuring it out. Robert Frost never read newspapers. "If something important happens, someone will tell me," he said. And there's the story of a coal miner, rescued after a week of total isolation and darkness following a cave-in. When interviewed, he said he'd done a lot of thinking down there, and had decided to cancel his newspaper subscription.

I feel archaic even talking about newspapers. They're dead—a few giants may linger on a while (but not long—the *Christian Science Monitor* suspended its daily print edition today). Local news may keep smalltown papers alive a little longer, although they're increasingly going to the Web. With this past summer, I've bowed out of mentoring interns on Indiana newspapers. I'm not disconsolate about the change, but I'm no longer qualified to advise students on how to proceed in the new media world, and they'd be crazy to plan careers on print newspapers.

Now typewriters, they might make a comeback. And if they do, you and Anne have a treasure trove. I would insert a typewritten page here, except that the Remington is in dire need of a ribbon transplant. When it gets one, you'll get a manually typed letter, promise.

Taking another break. Here's more confetti.

Sirius exclaiming in the morning sky.

Book nook: Believe I also promised to write about Norwegian novels. The first one I encountered this summer was *Out Stealing Horses* by Per Petterson—well written but a little post-modern for me. It left a lot of threads dangling (on purpose, I know). The second was *Berlin Poplars*, by Anne Ragde, a more traditional family saga, Dysfunctional Division. The former student who sent it to me lives in Trondheim, also the author's home. Ragde excels in describing occupations and milieus—she has either a truly strange resume, a varied group of friends, or a phenomenal talent for research. I learned about the undertaking business, dog training, pig farming, and gay life in Copenhagen, which is described in affectionate detail. "This is a book about some truly weird Norwegians," my correspondent wrote. "We're not all like this (just some of us)."

Hold on a little longer.

Stamps: One of the things I enjoy about your letters is all the postage stamps, old and new. I'm not a stamp collector, but like the color and variety. The Post Office does that part much better than in my youth, when it used to commemorate things like the Birth of the Poultry Industry. A common interest in stamps was one thing that drew my father, Jack, and David's father, Harry, together when Jack was living at the YMCA for a year in the 1930s. Jack once passed on a comment of Harry's to me, that a stamp "is only a stamp if it's been mailed. Until then, it's just a pretty picture." I think this applies, or should apply, to mail art also. In researching it on the Web, I find many varieties, some of which don't require that the art endure the vicissitudes of passage through the actual mail. Internet art may be wonderful, but it's not mail art, to my mind.

Odd, strange, and curious: Well, this whole letter could come under that heading. But I have to tell you that Karen and I had a brand-new experience last night. For 46 years we've been playing a game that requires each participant to guess a five-letter word chosen by the other. Last night, for the first time in 46 years, we found we had both chosen the same word: ingot. It's got to be a SIGN. We probably should draw out all our savings and convert them into gold bars (or at least half a gold bar).

THE END With much love.

To Dianne

I didn't plan it this way (and the Rem still needs a ribbon change), but the computer is off in another room cohabiting with the scanner. And I wanted to send a short, quick answer to your 10/26 letter, which arrived just after I mailed the previous.

I think the library show is a fine idea and am glad you're doing it. It will have a wonderful eclectic quality that will wow visitors, especially if they can actually touch things and carry the dolls around. The dolls should like that, too. Surely there can't be too much worry about damage—and if there is damage, well, it can be mended, can't it? You didn't exactly ask my opinion, but there it is anyway.

Also—without asking any kind of commitment this early—I'm charmed by the idea of showing up at the spring library show, and maybe even talking a little about the book (that is, as long as this can be done without putting me

in any kind of spotlight—could I just be Bill the Doll's visiting brother from Indiana?).

I'm touched by your reaction to the pictures. It's a different experience than publishing a book. The author always has copies around—too many unsold ones usually. It comes closer to the experience of sending poems to magazines, knowing it may be months before you hear anything, and then most probably it will be a rejection.

To Bill

Hello my dear Friend, thank you for your long letter and also the extra page that came after.

We are all thrilled with our president-elect and paid special attention to the INDIANA returns. THANK YOU for your politicking. We appreciate the time and energy you invested for all of us.

Everything is fine here. Anne and I are going to visit the Dubai family after Christmas and we are all going to Kenya together later.

Love, Dianne

The correspondence and the story do not end here, of course, but books must have an end, and it seems appropriate to close this one at the beginning of another trip.

My Uncle Bill collected memorable beginnings to novels. There are also memorable endings, but one of my favorites is both ending and beginning. It comes at the conclusion of *The Romany Rye*, George Borrow's tribute to his far-traveling Romany friends:

> "I shouldn't wonder," said I, as I proceeded rapidly along a broad causeway, in the direction of the east, "if Mr. Petulengro and Tawno Chickno came originally from India. I think I'll go there."

124

ACKNOWLEDGMENTS

We give special thanks to our families and friends who put up with hearing about this project over many months, and were pressed into service as unpaid editors and consultants. Without Karen Bridges, David Jenkins, and Anne Sears, it would never have happened.

Thanks also go to Dennis Cripe of the Pulliam School of Journalism at Franklin College for his endless patience in helping with Photoshop and imaging questions. Likewise to Susan Fleck, a former colleague of Bill's at the school, who helped with photographing outsize mail art.

Cover artists Lindsay Hadley and Tim Lisko did their usual fine job of creating an attractive wrapper for the book. Bill long ago decided he couldn't produce a book without these two talented designers.

We thank photographer Sue Nan Douglass for permission to reproduce from *Rubber Soul: Rubber Stamps and Correspondence Art* (University Press of Mississippi, 1996) the two pieces of Dianne's art that appear in "A Note at the Beginning" and on Page 15. Leila Salisbury, director of the University Press, was helpful in explaining copyright matters and pointing us to Sue Nan.

The title of this book is taken from a phrase in Pema Chödrön's book, *When Things Fall Apart: Heart Advice for Difficult Times.* Unless otherwise noted, all poetry is by the author, William Bridges.

Among those who assisted with information and advice were Jerry Reddan at Tangram Press, Bobby Bernshausen at VBW Publishing, and Matthew Kelsey.

And finally we thank the community of mail- and rubber-stamp artists, most of whom will never see their work in a book, but who keep making it and sending it out anyway, to the delight of the recipients.

11 MILLETT ROAD
SWAMPSCOTT
MA 01907